EVERYTHING YOU N[...]
BUYING Y[...]

LET'S
BUY A
HOUSE

TOM ARCHER

Cover image by: Ismail Derghal
Book design by: SWATT Books Ltd

Printed in the United Kingdom
First Printing, 2021

ISBN: 978-1-7398728-0-9 (Paperback)
ISBN: 978-1-7398728-1-6 (eBook)

Wilsie Publishing
Aldridge, West Midlands

Contents

Introduction

Buying a house can be a daunting prospect, especially if you have never done it before. It's most likely going to be the biggest purchase of your life and therefore it's critical to get it right. When I bought my first house in 2001, I had no idea what I was doing. I relied on my parents' advice and, to give you an idea how useful that advice was, they had last bought a house in 1982 and unfortunately for me things had changed a little since then.

I have gone on to buy more properties and undertaken this both on my own and with help from professionals. I learned that I still wasn't sure of the best or right way of successfully completing each transaction. This inspired me to become a licensed mortgage adviser, with the aim of properly understanding the house buying process thus ensuring I was receiving the right advice. Having this rounded knowledge has led to far smoother and easier (and less stressful!) house-buying journeys. As a result, I now offer this knowledge to all my mortgage clients. To make this information more widely available, I have now written this book. It is intended to be help you to obtain the right advice or to follow the right path if you choose to undertake doing it on your own. I sleep well at night knowing my clients have received the best advice, not only in obtaining the mortgage best suited to them but have also been able to really think through their choice of house, knowing it is right for them.

Most house purchases will require a mortgage and applying for a mortgage I would equate to driving a coach. A coach driver needs a specific licence to drive a coach for passengers on the road, just as a mortgage adviser needs a licence to provide mortgage advice for a client. If you're not qualified to drive a coach, I'm sure if you spent a little time in the driver's seat you could work out how to get the coach moving. Likewise, if you researched what is required for a mortgage you could probably work your way through a mortgage application.

Now, if you are on a straight, wide road with no sharp turns I am pretty sure most people could drive a coach from A to B with surprisingly little harm, damage or stress. Similarly, if you have no complications relating to your circumstances and do not stretch lenders' criteria and are willing to spend the time working out what is required, you could possibly get your mortgage application through to the point of gaining an offer from a lender.

However, not all roads are like this, and I recall a coach journey to the French Alps where I can assure you the roads were not straight or wide and our driver, along with every passenger, felt some sort of stress. Any wrong decision in steering or braking, any impacts from other drivers or weather, would have led to a fatal disaster in the form of a very long drop off the side of the road.

I really wish all mortgage applications were straightforward but unfortunately, straight, wide, uneventful roads are few and far between. Now, I am not saying all mortgage applications are as dramatic as a coach journey to the Alps, but like driving in the Alps sometimes it's easier and less stressful knowing someone who is licensed to drive is taking care of your journey from A to B or, in the case of house-buying, from first-time buyer to homeowner.

In this book I will accompany you on the whole of the journey involved in buying a house. My aim is to:

- ~ Help you to think about the types of property and location best suited to your needs
- ~ Lay out all the choices available to you of types of mortgage
- ~ Guide you to consider which type of mortgage suits your circumstances
- ~ Explain the mortgage application process
- ~ Provide details of all the parties involved and their responsibilities

Ultimately, by the end of this book I want you to be equipped with the knowledge and confidence to go out and buy a house, whether it be your first or if you are moving home. Everyone will have different objectives and needs, but by following my guide, I am confident that every reader will be able to find their perfect home *and* its accompanying most suitable mortgage.

Owning your own home can bring joy, independence and a sense of freedom and I can't wait to help you get there! So, sit down, grab a cuppa and dive in – your new home is waiting so *Let's Buy a House*.

Disclaimer

Please note that I am not a solicitor and therefore this book does NOT provide professional legal advice. It should be used just as a guide and an introduction to all aspects of buying a house. You should always seek professional advice – there are reminders about this throughout the book!

And, as a mortgage adviser, I feel that it is important to state this regulatory caveat in relation to all mortgages:

**YOUR HOME MAY BE REPOSSESSED IF YOU DO NOT
KEEP UP REPAYMENTS ON YOUR MORTGAGE**

Deciding you want to buy a house

Do you want to buy a house?

Everyone needs a roof over their head, but everyone's housing needs are different. From the day you were born until adulthood your housing need was most likely met by living with your parents or guardians, along with free meals, free heating and a TV package – happy days! However, those days don't, and probably shouldn't, last forever...

Where you go next is an important question to think about, because choosing to take on a mortgage will mean taking on the biggest debt you will ever have, so it's important you make the right decision.

Now, you may have a job that means you need to travel to different locations every six months, in which case renting would best suit your current housing needs. It may be that you simply don't feel ready to commit to an area or a person you buy with until you have tested the waters. You might like the idea of living in a city but until you hear those loud bars and restaurants late at night when you have an early start you won't know if it's right for you.

So, when deciding on your current housing needs, you need to consider all your options. These include owner occupation, privately renting or social renting. I will outline each of these, including a little background history.

Owner occupation

Before the twentieth century most families rented their property from private landlords. In the 1900s it was estimated that the UK housing stock was only about 10% owner occupied. Fast forward to the 2020s and nearly 70% of the UK housing stock is owner occupied.

This book is designed to guide you through the house buying process, so I won't go into much detail as to why this owner occupation shift has happened. However, it is worth analysing briefly why in the UK people prefer to buy their homes rather than to rent, and to do this I will give a brief history of the housing stock shift from privately rented to owner occupation.

During the eighteenth century the UK was the first country to experience industrialisation and mass migration from our rural towns to the cities and there were simply not enough houses to cope with demand. As a result, some of the larger companies sought to invest in house building to privately rent to their employees. However, many workers decided to provide for their own housing needs but needed a way of paying for their property in a way that they could afford. And so, the world's first financial institution specifically set up for lending money for land and property purchase was set up in Birmingham by a gentleman called Richard Ketley. Ketley's Building Society was proudly founded in 1775.

Building societies were run on a local basis and originated as self-help not-for-profit organisations. As a way of funding house purchases, building societies proved to be hugely successful, and right up until the early 1980s most residential mortgages were being offered through this route.

Successive UK governments have also contributed to the acceleration of the shift towards home ownership. Right up until 1999 tax relief on mortgage interest was made available to encourage owner occupation.

Up until 1984, those who chose to have an endowment mortgage (covered later in this book) had the option to claim Life Assurance Premium Relief

(LARP) on the premiums they were paying to a life assurance company. This again made it appealing to be a homeowner.

During the 1980s the promotion of home ownership was an explicit government policy which led to the Housing Act 1980, giving public sector tenants the right to buy their council house. This often came with generous discounts based on how long the tenant had lived there.

Now, as owner occupation was increasing this was reducing the availability of property to rent. This was compounded by the introduction of the Rents Act 1969 and 1974 which, while they gave powerful rights to tenants by making it more difficult for landlords to regain vacant possession, they came with the unintended consequence of landlords responding by increasing rents to compensate for the higher risks of letting their property. The result was a sharp decline in the availability of private rental properties.

All these factors led to home ownership becoming the most desirable option for many from the 1970s right up to the present day. Having said that, probably the most powerful incentive has been the astonishing upward trend in house prices in the past 50 years. No other asset has proved to be such a great way to protect oneself against inflation.

For over 50 years the general trend in residential prices has been upwards, although along the way there have been some major price corrections such as the slumps of 1991-92 and 2008-09... and who knows when the next one might be? Despite such slumps many people view their house as their most important physical asset and a source of wealth for future generations. As a result, in the UK in particular, we see a huge amount of trading up, using the equity in a house to buy ever bigger and more valuable houses. This is unlike many other European countries where people see purchasing a house as for life and tend not to trade up.

So, if owner occupation has become the accepted method for providing our housing needs, do we need to look at alternatives? Well, yes, it really is important to consider all other options before committing to owner occupation, so here is a brief look at these.

Social rented housing

The social rented sector is mainly made up of council houses rented from local authorities. This of course has steadily declined due to right-to-buy government policies during the 1970s, making it increasingly difficult to find a local authority house to rent. At its peak in the early 1980s, social housing, fuelled by a huge housebuilding boom after both world wars, made up one third of the housing stock – by 2020 this has shrunk to half that level.

Much of the diminished stock of social housing has now been transferred by local councils to private sector not-for-profit housing associations, often run by volunteers or a small number of staff. However, in whoever's hands the social rented housing stock lies, the waiting list to secure such accommodation, and the narrow qualification criteria needed, make this a difficult and unlikely route to pursue.

Private rented housing

Privately rented housing is on the rise. Following the decline in the 1960s and '70s mentioned above, the government realised it needed to reverse this trend and introduced measures to stimulate the private rental market. The Shorthold Tenancy Agreement was created by the Housing Act 1985. This meant the landlord could now fix the duration of the tenancy and the notice required by either party. The tenant was also protected, under certain circumstances, from being evicted. Most importantly however, tenants could no longer create indefinite rights of occupation.

Another significant factor which has helped the return of the private rented sector is the growth of buy-to-let mortgages. This has given investors the opportunity to mortgage an investment property based on rental incomes supporting the mortgage application. Also available is a let-to-buy option. This is for people who want to move home but can't sell their current property to release the equity. They keep their current property and rent it out. These are sometimes referred to as consumer buy-to-lets or even as accidental landlords, as their circumstances have resulted in them becoming landlords rather than by choice.

So, given that private rented housing is back in the mainstream, is it right for you? There is already a Generation Rent emerging, those who have left the family home but either through choice (an enjoyment of the lack of responsibility for the maintenance of a property) or necessity (the escalation in house prices and the difficulty of saving for a deposit). Also, as mentioned in the Introduction, there may be many other reasons why renting suits your lifestyle or job situation compared with owner occupation. Either way, the breadth of choice and the availability of private rented housing means that it can be a useful step along the way to owner occupation, giving you the time and space to work out your longer-term housing needs compared with previous generations perhaps faced with the starker choice of continuing to live with mum and dad or needing to buy.

Tax

That has now summarised the different types of housing solutions available to fulfil our housing needs. You may have noticed the government has a lot of influence over the housing market. Still today, the government plays a role through its economic and social policies. We are now going to focus on the owner occupier housing need, as this book is aimed at helping you buy a house.

Now, it's never too long before we mention tax when it comes to money, and this book is no different. I must make it clear that I am not a tax adviser and therefore throughout this book I am NOT offering tax advice! However, the tax implications in relation to property ownership are potentially significant and it is important that you make yourself aware of them. More detailed information can be found on the Gov.UK website.

Stamp Duty

A key tax you need to be aware of when buying a house, and one which seems to change on a regular basis, is Stamp Duty Land Tax (SDLT). HM Revenue and Customs practice and the law relating to taxation are complex and subject to individual circumstances and changes which cannot be foreseen. At the time of writing this book you are liable to pay stamp duty when you purchase a property or a piece of land which costs more than £125,000. The amount you pay is based on certain thresholds or bands as a percentage of the purchase price and may also be affected by your circumstances. For example, first time buyers currently benefit from a certain amount of stamp duty relief when they buy their first house.

As an illustration, let's take a first-time buyer purchasing their first home for £300,000 or less. They will pay no SDLT, so this represents a saving of up to £5,000 compared with a non-first-time buyer in the same situation. Where the purchase price is over £300,000 but does not exceed £500,000, they will pay 5% on the amount above £300,000. First time buyers purchasing a house over £500,000 will pay normal stamp duty rates and not qualify for any relief, but, hey, being in that sort of position as a first-time buyer, you may not be that bothered! An important aspect to note is that if a couple are buying a house where one person is a first-time buyer but the other is not you will NOT qualify for the first-time buyer stamp duty relief.

At the other end of the scale, a buyer who currently owns a property they reside in and do not plan to sell when they move on to another residential property (let-to-buy), will incur an additional stamp duty charge.

For general info on SDLT go to www.gov.uk/stamp-duty-land-tax

For a more detailed calculator, go to www.tax.service.gov.uk/calculate-stamp-duty-land-tax/#/intro

Then fill out the boxes or ask your financial adviser for help.

Here is the current position for stamp duty, as at November 2021:

Minimum property purchase price	Maximum property purchase price	Stamp Duty rate (applies only to the part of the property price falling within each band)
£0	£125,000	0%
£125,001	£250,000	2%
£250,001	£925,000	5%
£925,001	£1.5 million	10%
Over £1.5 million		12%

Example: *if you were not a first-time buyer and were to purchase a property for £300,000:*

0% on the first £125,000 = £0

2% on the next £125,000 = £2500

5% on the next £50,000 = £2500

Total stamp duty liability: £5,000

*First-time buyers would pay £0 in this example.

UK governments seem to like making changes to stamp duty, whether it be in buyers' favour, as with the stamp duty holiday given during the Covid-19 pandemic, or changes on a regular basis to the bands and rates. For example, with effect from April 2016, buyers of additional residential properties such as second homes or buy-to-let properties now pay a 3% surcharge over the standard rate for each band. This increased rate applies to properties costing £40,000 or more ie pretty much every property!

A word of warning: if you are selling your current residential property to move into another and there is a delay in selling but you complete the purchase of your new house you will be liable to pay the higher stamp duty rates as you will (however briefly) own two properties. You can apply for a refund of the additional tax you paid if you sell or give away your previous home within 3 years of buying your new house.

Council Tax

Council Tax is an annual fee the local authority charges to provide a broad range of local services. We need to consider Council Tax when we look at the affordability of owning or renting a house, as you will have to pay it as an owner occupier or as a tenant, social or private. Since 2000, there has been a significant steady increase in the amount payable as Council Tax and therefore it now represents a sizeable monthly outlay.

The amount you will pay will vary depending on the value of your home and where you live. Most local authorities will have the banding costs on their website but do not be shy to ask the sellers what they are currently paying when you are viewing a property. This is a question that often gets missed.

Inheritance Tax

Inheritance Tax is a tax on the estate of a deceased person, the estate being property, money and possessions.

At the time of writing this book, there is usually no Inheritance Tax liability if an estate has a total value below £325,000 or if you leave everything above the £325,000 threshold to your spouse, civil partner, a charity or a community amateur sports club. It's important to mention this due to the continued rise in house prices. Some owner occupiers do not realise how much their estate is worth and seeking financial advice is important when planning your estate.

We have now discussed the different solutions to housing needs and the taxation involved with being an owner occupier. Before moving on, now is a good time to reflect and think what type of housing would best you in your current circumstances.

Next, we are going to discuss the different types of borrowers and lenders.

Borrowers and lenders

Not many buyers can afford to buy a house with cash (cash buyer) which means they will have to take out a mortgage. So, what is a mortgage? Well, before we rush into that let's clear up the terms of who is who, as it is easy to confuse them.

The borrower is you, as you are borrowing the money, and the lender is the bank, building society etc as they are going to lend you the money.

A mortgage is a secured loan, whereby a borrower (you) obtains finance from a lender (the bank etc) by offering a property as security for the loan. If you are unable to pay the loan the lender can then use the property as security to pay back the loan.

Lenders need to cater for a wide range of mortgage needs and so have developed a range of mortgage products to suit different types of buyer. We will discuss later different mortgage needs but for now we are going to look at the types of buyers.

First-time buyers

A first-time buyer is someone who is buying their first residential property and has never owned a freehold or had a leasehold interest in a residential property in the UK or abroad*.

__Important point to note:__ some lenders choose to class someone who has not had a mortgage or owned a house for more than 3 years as a first-time buyer. However, this is just various lenders' criteria and should not be used as a classification for tax purposes.

A first-time buyer differs from other borrowers in the sense that they will not have accumulated any equity from a previous property. This contrasts with a home mover who hopefully would have either paid off a certain amount of their current mortgage or have seen their property gain in value or both. This means the first-time buyer will have had to save a deposit using income, or as we see more and more, rely on the bank of mom and dad to gift a deposit.

First-time buyers are critically important to the housing market. As discussed earlier, we have a tendency to trade up in the UK and without first-time buyers coming into the property market home movers cannot trade in their smaller properties for larger ones. What doesn't help a first-time buyer is the seemingly relentless increases in house prices. They are confronted with this just at the point in their career where they may be earning the least. With that in mind, lenders are increasingly offering 90% to 95% loan-to-value (LTV) mortgages, meaning home buyers, and especially first-time buyers, are able to buy a house with just a 5% deposit.

It is worth mentioning the risk to lenders, as a lender will want to assess the risk to their money before lending. They will assess the borrower and the property being offered up as security to arrive at a decision as to whether their money is safe. First-time buyers nearly always represent a higher risk, as they often provide a lower deposit, have no track record of servicing a debt, and are on lower incomes than more mature borrowers.

As a first-time buyer, it is important to be clear on your budget before you look at potential houses, as there will most likely be very little room to increase affordability.

Home mover

A home mover has a house to sell and a house to buy. This means they may have money from the sale of their house (the equity) to use towards the purchase of the new house. Do not take that equity for granted though as during 2008-2009 we saw house prices fall to a point where some homeowners were left in negative equity which meant they owed more on their mortgage than the new value of their house. Following the 2008-2009 financial crisis, a swathe of reform has resulted in the financial regulators tightening up on lending rules. This has meant that for some homeowners who purchased their house prior to the crisis, who were granted a large mortgage to do so, can now no longer reach the same level of lending to move to a similar size or larger house. In some cases, they have not been able to replace the mortgage on their current house. They have become "mortgage trapped".

What is positive for the home mover is that they have built up a credit history and have demonstrated how they have conducted the repayment of their current mortgage. This of course is a double-edged sword. If you have missed payments on your mortgage the lender may see you as higher risk and not have the appetite to lend to you.

Another important point to make is that the home mover's circumstances may have changed since they first bought their house. For example, you may have had children and one parent may have reduced their hours to look after them. If your income has been reduced, lenders may not be able to lend you as much as they did before. Or you may have taken out a large loan to finance a car, which may affect the amount a lender can lend.

It is just as important to a home mover to check affordability before looking for properties as it is for first-time buyers. Make sure you have updated your current financial position and checked the lenders' criteria. Your financial adviser can help with this.

Right to buy

A right-to-buy property is a property belonging to local authorities, councils, and registered social landlords. Since 1980 most council tenants have been allowed to buy their council house at a discount depending on eligibility. You can find out if you are eligible here on the government website https://righttobuy.gov.uk/am-i-eligible/eligibility-quiz/

The discount will depend on how long you have been a council tenant and does not require you to have lived in the same home for the whole time you have been a tenant.

If, once you have bought the right-to-buy property, you decide to sell within the first 10 years of ownership you will need to offer it back to the original landlord ie the council. If the landlord does not agree to buy the property back after 8 weeks, you are then free to offer it on the open market. If you decide to sell within 5 years of ownership you may have to pay back some or all the discount you have received.

Shared ownership

Housing associations offer private shared ownership schemes at a local level. You buy a share, normally 25%, 50% or 75% of the house, and the association owns the remaining share, which you will pay rent on. Usually, the terms in the lease allow the tenant to buy more of the association's share during ownership. This is known as staircasing, right up to 100% ownership. The rent you pay should be factored into affordability.

You can sell your shared ownership property usually at the same split you currently own and rent, and the new owner can carry on with the staircasing if they so wish.

There is also a government-backed shared ownership scheme which works under similar principles.

If you are a first-time buyer of a shared ownership property, you used to own your home but cannot afford to buy one now, or you are an existing shared owner, you may be eligible depending on your household income.

If you are aged 55 or over, you can buy up to 75% of your home through the Older People's Shared Ownership Scheme. Under this scheme, once you own 75% you will not pay rent on the rest.

Borrowers with adverse credit

Adverse credit could be anything from a missed phone bill payment to bankruptcy. There are occasions where buyers do not even realise that they are in any adverse credit until a mortgage application is declined and they check their credit file. It is always worth checking your credit file, especially as most offer free reports for the first 30 days with the option to cancel the subscription if you choose to.

Some lenders understand that life happens and that anyone can suffer financial difficulties. However, it is likely that they will want to see that you have bounced back from those financial difficulties or have rectified the issue causing the adverse credit.

A lender needs to be confident in the ability of a borrower to repay the mortgage once it has been issued. Your financial track record is so important. It's fair to say that if a potential borrower has a loan for, say, £10,000 and has missed the last 3 months' payments there is a strong chance they could miss payments on the £150,000 mortgage they are now applying for. Now, there are adverse lenders out there who may be willing to lend in certain circumstances to people with such a chequered financial history. However, you must think carefully about your decision before you borrow money secured against the house you will live in! If you can't keep up with your current credit commitments, what chance when you have a great big mortgage payment to pay each month as well?

If you have an adverse credit history, you will need to check the lender criteria before making an application; a financial adviser can help you with this.

Guarantors

Some lenders offer the opportunity for a personal guarantee to be given for someone who is creditworthy but has a low income and is applying for a mortgage.

A guarantee is a written contract whereby one person, normally a relative (Mom or Dad) takes on the responsibility to repay the debt or mortgage, in this case for another person. It doesn't mean the guarantor will need to pay the monthly payments each month but it does mean that if the borrower falls short on payments or defaults on the mortgage then the guarantor will be called upon to repay the debt.

A guarantor is urged to consider this arrangement carefully as it is a legally binding contract. The lender will probably require the guarantor to seek legal advice so that the guarantor cannot claim undue influence as a way in the future to try and escape a claim.

This may sound like a useful alternative way to secure a mortgage. However, the mortgage will then be assessed based on the guarantor's circumstances. If we use the example of a parent being the guarantor, we need to think, if they have an existing mortgage, can they afford two mortgages in the event of a default? You may think, that is OK, my parents are mortgage free, so that will be fine. But are they mortgage free because they are retired and only have a small pension income, thus reducing the amount they can borrow? Or are they at an age whereby you can only take out a shorter-term mortgage, say just 10 years, because the lender will only lend up to the age of 70 and your parents are 60. The monthly payments would then be far higher on a 10-year term mortgage compared with a 30-year term one.

Not all lenders offer guarantor mortgages, so check their criteria beforehand or ask your financial adviser.

Lenders

Banks
The larger retail banks started to become major players of the mortgage markets in the 1980s when the financial markets were deregulated. Before then the building societies arranged a recommended interest rate to keep rates artificially low, which made the mortgage market unattractive to the banks.

The larger retail banks are multinational organisations offering a full range of financial services. During the 1990s and beyond, larger banks started to offer a 'one-stop shop' approach to banking and finance. They set out to encourage their customers to enter into multiple relationships under one roof. A bank could now provide a customer a current account, a mortgage, credit cards, personal loans, life assurance and general insurance.

So, how do banks finance a mortgage so you can borrow it? Well, they borrow it. Banks borrow money from the wholesale markets. The wholesale markets have their own interest rates which means the costs affecting the banks borrowing may affect the cost of your borrowing.

Between 1989-2000, some banks used to be building societies but decided to remove their mutual status so that they could become public limited companies. By 2008 every building society that went public had either been sold to a conventional bank or nationalised. This has resulted in the remaining building societies being slightly different when it comes to the way they fund their finances.

Building societies
Building societies are financial institutions owned by their members, savers and borrowers. They are not limited companies like the banks, but they do share some of the characteristics of limited companies, including

separate legal personality and limited liability. They are regulated under the Building Society Acts 1986 and 1997.

Building societies are obliged to raise 50% of their funding from retail sources, which means that most of the money borrowed when mortgaging with a building society is coming from personal savings accounts. This somewhat protected the building societies during the 2008/9 financial crisis, as they are limited as to how much they can lend depending on how much their members are saving. Also, as building societies are not floated on the stock market, they did not run the risk of falling share prices.

Another characteristic of a building society is that 75% of their commercial assets must be mortgages secured on land for residential use. This keeps building societies wedded to their roots as savings and mortgage institutions. However, the Building Society Act 1986 did give the opportunity for building societies to expand their operations into mainstream banking services.

Before deregulation in the 1980s, building societies accounted for 70% of the total mortgage lending in the UK. This changed drastically when the main banks and other financial institutions entered the mortgage market.

As for today, from a borrower's point of view there is very little difference in the features and benefits of mortgage lending from a bank or from a building society. However, building societies stress the benefits of being a mutual institution and seek to differentiate themselves from other players.

Insurance companies

Insurance companies used to confine themselves to lending funds to employees only. However, in the 1970s, during a time of increasing house prices, the building societies began to struggle to service bigger loans or attract enough savings to service the mortgage demand, so the insurance companies began to offer top-up loans to the public.

Some insurance companies today have become their own banks, usually internet and telephone based. The lending is funded by the parent life assurance company and by their savers.

Local authorities

At one time, the building societies biggest competitors were local authorities, who were often prepared to lend on properties the building societies did not have the appetite for, such as inner-city dilapidated houses, flats and maisonettes. They were also funding the right-to-buy schemes.

However, there have now been significant reductions in local authority spending in recent years which has led to most local authorities ceasing to offer new mortgage loans. Indeed, some have sold on their mortgage loans to other lenders to try to recoup their money quicker.

Employee schemes

Some employers may offer mortgage lending to their employees. These include banks, building societies and insurance companies and, as they are lending to their employees, they may offer favourable interest rates. Where some employers may not be able to offer mortgages, they may be able to offer subsidies to reduce the overall cost of the mortgage – this is often available in areas where living costs are high. There are implications from these schemes relating to National Insurance Contributions, for employers and for employees. More information on this can be found on the government website: www.gov.uk/hmrc-internal-manuals/national-insurance-manual/nim02240

Mortgage intermediaries/brokers

Given the enormous choice of mortgages and the complexities of the different lending criteria each lender puts in place, using a mortgage intermediary or broker can be an invaluable way to gain advice on finding the best lender for your needs. Most mortgage brokers will offer a comprehensive service:

~ researching the most suitable mortgage for you in your current circumstances
~ dealing with your mortgage application
~ applying for the mortgage
~ packaging the documents required correctly for the lender, which will require underwriting
~ liaise with estate agents and solicitors during the complex house purchase process

~ having an ongoing relationship with the lender to see your application go through to offer and then completion and then to you receiving the keys to your new home.

Mortgage intermediaries can take the hassle and much of the uncertainty out of the mortgage application process and have tools available to recommend a lender suitable for your circumstances.

There is a key difference between using an intermediary and going direct to a bank or building society. A mortgage intermediary will be able to look at multiple lenders and their lending criteria, whereas going to a bank or building society you will only be using their criteria which may not always be favourable to your circumstances. An intermediary could save you a lot of time and be more efficient when dealing with estate agents and solicitors.

Some intermediaries charge a fee, although others do not. Either way, an intermediary should always explain what their fee structure is and what it provides before you engage with their advice process.

An intermediary may be independent or part of a network or mortgage club. An independent intermediary must have processes and recording systems set up which comply with FCA (Financial Conduct Authority) requirements, and these can be expensive. They will also need to provide a training and competence scheme, IT systems and support staff to ensure all requirements are met. A solution for the intermediary to these requirements is to join a network who will provide the infrastructure for compliance with all the regulations. A network could be whole-of-market ie provide access to a wide range of lenders, or may use a selective panel of lenders. The number of lenders available will depend on the network and what they offer.

Help to Buy

Help to Buy loans were introduced by the government for first-time buyers and for home movers to buy specifically a new-build home. However, Help to Buy is, at the time of writing, only available to first-time buyers. The clue is in the title – the scheme is designed to stimulate the housing market for new borrowers by making it easier for them to buy. Under the scheme, borrowers are able to take out a mortgage on a reduced portion of the property, 75% instead of the typical 90% or even 95%. Borrowers provide 5% of the value with their own funds as a deposit, with the Help to Buy scheme providing the remaining 20% (40% in London) and 20% being the maximum contribution available outside of London. There is no requirement to use the full allowance – for example, if you wanted to contribute 10% to the deposit you can still mortgage 75% and then use the Help to Buy scheme to fund just 15% of the purchase price.

Fees on the Help to Buy scheme loan are not charged for the first five years but then a fee of 1.75% of the loan's value is charged in the sixth year. In subsequent years the fee is increased in relation to the retail price index.

When the Help to Buy scheme was introduced in 2003 people were eligible to buy a house up to £600,000 across the UK. However, since April 2021 and up to at least March 2023 there will be a price cap depending on the area in which the house purchase is being made. This can vary from London remaining at £600,000 to the North-East having a cap of £186,100. Just as with Stamp Duty, Help to Buy is likely to be subject to future amendments by the government, so consult the Gov.UK site for up-to-date information.

The Help to Buy scheme is for residential purposes only so you cannot then sublet your house if you have used the scheme to buy your house.

Your financial adviser can help you to assess your eligibility for the scheme.

YOUR HOME MAY BE REPOSSESSED IF YOU DO NOT KEEP UP REPAYMENTS ON YOUR MORTGAGE

Decide on a budget

So, we have got to the point where you have decided YES, I want to become a homeowner. This is an exciting moment, but potentially a daunting one too, so this guide is here to help.

You may be keen to get onto Rightmove or your local estate agents' websites so you can start imagining yourself in the houses displayed. However, before rushing into that, there is a critically important job to do first and that is looking in detail at the matter of affordability. I am amazed how many buyers start viewing houses without even knowing how much they can afford.

Knowing your budget will set your expectations where they need to be and save you a lot of time by refining your search to your budget. Everybody loves browsing for their dream house, and there's nothing wrong with doing that for fun, but when this is now the beginning of a journey towards a real purchase, it's time to focus!

As discussed earlier, most buyers need to borrow the money to finance a house purchase. Affordability for a cash buyer is simple arithmetic – how much cash do you have minus any Stamp Duty due and any other fees such as legal fees, estate agency fees if any, moving costs etc.

However, affordability for someone who wants a mortgage requires considering a number of factors.

your income is assessed, what types of incomes
ʌle and what proportion of those income streams are
ɘ ie some lenders will allow the inclusion of 100% of
ʌe payments, while some only allow 50%. Will your income
ᴜ ɟe over time? Someone at the beginning of a professional
career is likely to enjoy future increases in salary. Conversely,
someone taking out a mortgage in later life may want to reduce
their hours, and therefore their salary, towards the end of the
mortgage. What evidence is required to support your income?
A payslip may be sufficient to prove your basic income, but, for
example, an annual bonus may require 3 years of evidence. If
you are self-employed how many years accounts do you need?
All lender requirements are different but take the time from the
outset to gather as much documentation as possible. If you are
reliant on a notoriously slow HR department in your company for
this, get a request in early!

~ **Expenditure:** Here is where lenders get personal! They can
ask for detailed information about your lifestyle and your
expenditure! Each may have different ways of looking into how
your expenditure is assessed. Again, think carefully about all your
committed expenditure such as loan payments, as well as basic
essential expenditure such as utility bills, food and household
expenditure, along with your basic quality of living costs. Stepping
back and taking stock of all this is a useful (and possibly sobering!)
analysis to do at any time, but prior to jumping into committing
to the largest loan of your life, it's essential!

~ How future interest rates are considered – we cannot assume
interest rates will always remain at the historically low levels they
have been at in the 2010s and early 2020s. Would you be able to
afford your mortgage if interest rates increased?

~ What calculations are going to be used to determine whether the
loan is affordable? Some lenders offer larger loans for those with
incomes over certain thresholds; some lenders reduce the amount
they will lend if you have a debt in the background which is a
certain ratio of your income.

Along with auditing and record-keeping, a lender has a huge amount to consider when assessing affordability. In turn, not all lenders are the same in how they assess affordability, which is why it may be advantageous to speak to a financial adviser who can undertake research for you and work out how much a lender is likely to offer to lend you. Such advisers can then help to gather all the relevant evidence about your income and expenditure and submit a mortgage application in a way that they know will be in line with that lender's policies, thus maximising your chances of success.

Let's now go into some more detail regarding income and expenditure.

Types of income

A borrower's income can derive from several sources:

~ Basic income or salary if employed, or income from trading if self-employed
~ Overtime
~ Bonuses
~ Commission
~ Trust income
~ Pension income
~ Maintenance payments income
~ State benefits

A lender will consider the income received, whether it be a single application or joint, and, as discussed before, they will assess each part of the income based on their policies or criteria. A guarantor's income will also be assessed if there is one. If your income is volatile ie you can earn double your income in commission one month and then zero the next, the lender will need to be confident in a level of consistency of this income stream over a period of time. If unsatisfied about this, they may disregard this income altogether. If not volatile but varying, the lender may take an average over a certain period ie over 3 years or 3 months depending on the nature and volatility of the income. It is safe to say that most lenders will use 100% of your basic income.

Employed borrowers' PAYE

There are several different types of employed borrowers, the most common being an open-ended employment contract where either party to the contract has the option to terminate the contract subject to an agreed period of notice. If the contract is for more than 16 hours work per week, the employee benefits from significant protection under employment law once they have served a minimum of 12 months.

Part-time employees work a specified number of hours each week for an employer and can of course have more than one part-time job which adds up to full-time hours. A lender will happily take into account any and all relevant income from part-time work.

Fixed term contracts are becoming more popular with both employees and employers. These give the option to terminate a contract after a specified period. This type of contract is accommodated by lenders, but they will want to see consistency when assessing affordability. Fixed term contracted employees will need to show that they either have had a solid history of securing regular fixed term contracts or that their current contract is for a significant period of time and not coming to an end shortly.

Temporary workers usually work through an agency but can also work direct for an employer on a temporary basis, such as in a retail shop over the busy Christmas period. If you prefer the flexibility of working as a temporary employee, you will need to consider how you will provide evidence for the consistency of your income. Most lenders will ask for 12 months proof of income and will not want to see any gaps within that 12-month period, but it's always best to check each lender's criteria first.

While lenders may see contracted employees as being able to provide the most dependable, consistent level of income and therefore present the least difficulties in obtaining a mortgage, it should also be considered that the fixed term contractor may be remunerated highly for their services and that if a fixed term contract is terminated, they are no more likely to stay unemployed than a person made redundant from another type of contract.

Self-employed sole traders and unlimited partnerships

Being self-employed means working for yourself rather than for an employer, although even under that definition you may work for the same company day-in day-out. You may be, for example, a bricklayer contracted to the same building firm on an ongoing basis, and yet you would still classify as self-employed to a lender.

Depending on the size of their business, a sole trader may or may not be able to use audited accounts as evidence of income. However, all self-employed persons are required to submit an annual tax return declaring their income, and this can be the foundation for evidence of income.

If you use an accountant to produce a set of accounts and want to use these accounts to support your mortgage application, your accountant will need to be a member of a recognised supervisory body – they will need to be either a chartered accountant or a certified accountant.

If you are relying on your tax return as evidence of income, or you or your accountant completes a rudimentary income statement, this can be confirmed in a form SA302 issued by HMRC in February or March each year. However, this is an annual submission, and, depending on when you apply for a mortgage, the income you declare could be nearly a year out of date. Due to this, some lenders will allow you until October to submit accounts for the tax year which has ended in the most recent April. This is ahead of the HMRC deadline of the January following that tax year, so it is worth ensuring you are organised with your tax return information.

HMRC will also issue a tax year overview which will show £0 when you have paid your tax bill, and this can be useful evidence of the taxable income you have submitted.

Most lenders will want to see 2 to 3 years' worth of accounts or 2 to 3 years' SA30s and tax year overviews. They may also require an accountant's reference. Depending on the nature of the business or the volatility of the income they may also require evidence of a business plan. However, an accountant's reference can normally satisfy this.

The lender will be looking at how your income has changed over the past 3 years. If you have had a steady increase each year, they may use an average of the last two years or even just focus on the most recent year. However, if your income has decreased, they will most likely use the lower latest figures only and want to be reassured it won't continue to decrease.

All lenders assess self-employed income differently, so depending on your circumstances certain lenders could be more favourable than others which is why it important to research which lenders are available to you and their criteria – a financial adviser can help with this.

With the significant increase in self-employment in the UK some lenders have adapted their criteria by allowing only two years trading, and there are now lenders who will even allow just one year's trading, but these are few and far between.

Let's now explode the myth that lenders don't like lending or lend as much to self-employed borrowers. It's not true! It's just that the evidence of income needs to be laid out and explained in a different way.

I answer the employed income v self-employed income debate in this way: "First, fair enough, you only have to be employed for a short period of time to obtain a mortgage, but you most likely will still have to provide evidence that you have worked for over 12 months or have a good reason not to have, like undertaking childcare. Secondly, if your self-employed average earnings for the last three or two years, depending on the lender, are the same as an employed person the lender will most likely assess the value of that income in the same way ie if I am contracted to earn £30,000 per annum employed or my average earnings self-employed are £30,000 per annum lenders will treat this in the same way."

One of the benefits of being self-employed is that you can offset costs you cannot usually offset when employed, so even if it may look like you are earning less on paper, you may be financially better off – your 'affordability' score is therefore better.

My point is that lenders do not favour employed or self-employed – they simply have to be sure they have been satisfied with proof of income now and in the future, which may happen to be easier for an employed borrower than a self-employed borrower. However, if presented in the correct way to a lender, self-employment income need not be any barrier to obtaining a mortgage.

Special attention will be taken into consideration when lenders look at mortgage applications from a borrower who is part of a partnership. HMRC documentation will be the same as those of a sole trader. Each partner will be individually assessed on their share of the profits in the business and receive a form SA302 each year.

However, each partner in any partnership, during the course of their work is jointly and severally liable for their obligations under the Partnerships Act 1890 and also liable for torts (negligence) under the Civil Liability (contributions) Act 1978. In short, this means all partners are liable for all the debts. Even a new partner who has come into the partnership and has nothing to do with any of the accumulated debts will now be liable for them because limited liability does not apply: it is a personal obligation. This principle therefore extends to the mortgage when it is granted, as partners are responsible for their own debt whilst sharing responsibility for each other's debt as well.

Limited liability partnerships and limited companies

Limited liability partnerships and limited companies have a separate legal identity which means they have their own liabilities and own assets; in both cases they can sue and be sued in their own name in a court of law. Limited liability partnerships are therefore very similar to private limited companies and can be seen as a sort of hybrid of a traditional partnership and a limited company.

Limited companies can be either private or public. Most limited companies are private. Public companies may issue shares on the stock exchange and therefore their shares can be bought and sold by a wider range of interested parties.

Income from limited liability partnerships comes from each partner's share of the profits, similar to sole traders.

As a director of a limited company, you will most likely receive a salary and a dividend as income. Both can be used by a lender when assessing affordability. Some lenders choose to use salary and net profit from a director's accounts when assessing income. This is favourable for directors who may have left money in the business and have chosen not to draw it as a salary or dividend. A lender will require two- or three-years accounts or the same SA302 and tax year overviews to evidence income.

Expenditure

So, we have told lenders what money is coming in – we now need to tell them what is going out.

We will also discuss the impact of your credit score, as assessed by credit bureaux, as this has an influence on lenders too.

It is important to state that it is a serious offence to deliberately conceal relevant information from lenders. You need to be open, honest and transparent about all your credit commitments! From an adviser's point of view there is simply no point in a borrower trying to conceal any credit commitments, as the lender during their assessment will check with a credit bureau and all current credit commitments will be available to view. Usually there is a history of six years' information available. At the touch of a button, your current credit rating and history is available online! There is nowhere to hide!

When declaring your expenditure, the lender will want to consider loans, hire purchase, credit card and store card commitments. So many borrowers slip up here by forgetting the sofa they put on finance or the store card they took out to pay for a transaction. The best thing to do is to check your credit score and rating with a credit bureau before the lender does!

A credit bureau report shows you how your credit commitments have been managed. If you have missed any payments on a credit card, loan or any commitment, including phone bills, this will be highlighted, when and how much was missed. If you miss a payment for 6 consecutive months this can lead to you defaulting on an account. The default information will then be logged on your report. If you pay the default amount you will clear the default BUT it will still remain on your credit file for 6 years. If you do not pay it, it will remain unsettled. Unfortunately, even small missed payments can come back to haunt you, years later!

Put yourself in the lender's shoes: if you have missed 6 payments in the last 12 months on a loan for, let's say £5,000, what is the financial risk to them of lending you, say, £150,000 for a mortgage? It's high! Now, I am not saying you won't be able to get a mortgage in this scenario, but a lot of lenders won't have the appetite to lend, and the lenders who do, like a specialist adverse lender, may want a higher return for their risk in the form of higher interest rates or higher fees.

County court judgments (CCJs) are also reported on a credit report, again satisfied or unsatisfied. A CCJ is issued when someone takes court action saying you owe them money and you do not respond. Government guidelines state that if you pay a CCJ within one month you can get it removed from the register of judgments. Beware though – if you delay and pay after one month it will stay on the register for 6 years even though it is marked as satisfied.

Bankruptcy and insolvency will also appear on a credit file and a borrower who has ever been bankrupt must declare if they have been so, no matter how long ago. A solicitor's bankruptcy search later on in the legal process will highlight this so non-disclosure could result in a lender declining the application.

Missed payments or any adverse credit can affect your affordability rating. The lender may restrict the loan to value (LTV) being offered, so you now need to contribute a larger deposit. Be aware that when checking an online affordability calculator with a lender they will assume at that stage you are a low-risk borrower with no adverse credit. So, you won't know the exact amount a lender will lend until you submit an 'application in principle' (sometimes called a mortgage in principle or decision in principle). It is only after this that a credit bureau will be contacted to assess your credit file, and the assessment of this could then downgrade your affordability rating if there is some adverse credit history.

So, we have discussed committed expenditure, but what about your food bills, gym membership, or general spending money on all sorts of things such as entertainment or days out? Most lenders have built into their affordability assessment the average cost of living in local areas, and that is why some lenders ask for an area or postcode on their affordability calculator. On certain expenditure, lenders may ask for the amount you are spending and if this is below the average, they will use the higher figure. For example, if your travel costs are £40 per month but the average in your area of the UK are £50, the lender will use £50 in the affordability assessment.

Up to now we have discussed expenditure as information for the lender to use to assess affordability, but now you need to make your own honest assessment of affordability. Although a lender may offer to lend you an amount which far exceeds your expectations you need to resist the temptation to grab it until you have thought in detail about your monthly/

annual budget and your lifestyle. Yes, you want to get a mortgage, but do you want to sacrifice your current standard of living to do so and take every pleasure away just to pay the mortgage? Itemise a detailed budget for all your outgoings and decide which must stay and which you can afford to cut back on. If there are extras you are willing to sacrifice like a top-of-the-range TV package then, great, go ahead but if you're the kind of person who cannot do without the sports package then let's keep it in your budget.

Below is a table of expenditure for you to fill out – this exercise may feel like a bit of a chore, but I guarantee it will save you a great deal of pain and disappointment in the future. I also guarantee that, if you have not done it before, you will surprised, shocked even, by the results! Only by standing back and coolly and objectively itemising your expenditure will you work out a true affordability figure – and so much better for you to do that AHEAD of the lender doing it! And if there are two of you conducting this exercise, itemised as 'Borrower No1' and 'Borrower No2' in the table, then being honest with each other is vital too!

A quick tip – when I assess affordability for my clients, I always take 25% off their budgets for emergencies, so please use 25% of your budget to save for an emergency fund! There is no set amount you should have in your emergency fund, but a good starting point would be 3 months' worth of bills.

Start by putting your monthly net income in at the top – that's what you are left with after your deductions such as tax and national insurance. If you receive any benefits remember to add them in too. If you are self-employed, you can divide your net profit into twelve months to give you a figure. Remember, all income, even pension income or maintenance payments if you receive it, should be included.

Now, this is only a template, and you may have other expenditure not listed, so just add it in the blank boxes available. Again, you are entering average monthly figures in each expenditure box. Please note: the bills and property overheads are not what you are paying now, but what you expect to pay in your new house. As a good start-point, you can find a handy list of household costs on Zoopla but do not take those figures as 100% correct.

Other costs such as car insurance and loan payments you will know, as they will be current expenditure. If you are renting now, of course you do not need to add the rent as your rent will cease when you move into your new home.

	Borrower No1	Borrower No2	Benefits	Other	Total
Net Income					

	Borrower No1	Borrower No2	Total
Council Tax			
Water Rates			
Gas			
Electricity			
TV Licence			
Internet Services			
Mobile Phone			
Car Insurance			
Car Tax			
Petrol			
Buildings & Contents Insurance			
Life Insurances			
Income Protection			
Loan Payments			
Credit Cards			
Spending Money			
Food			
Gym			
Holiday			
Child Care Costs			
Other			
Other			
Other			
Other			

Total Expenditure	

So, we now have figures for total income and total expenditure. Take the expenditure away from the income to give you a gross budget. Be sitting down when you make this calculation 😊.

Total Income	
Minus Expenditure	
Gross Budget	

As discussed, I now recommend taking 25% away from your budget for emergencies. So, Gross Budget − 25% = Your Available Budget to pay for your mortgage. (If you don't have a % button on your calculator you can multiply your budget figure by 0.75 to take off 25% of your budget). Now, this is not a target figure that you are now aiming at. You don't have to find a mortgage that is the equivalent of this net budget figure each month, but you need to know this figure so you can ensure your mortgage payments do not go above this.

Gross Budget	
Minus 25%	
Net Budget	

So, how is this net budget figure looking? It is probably lower than the one you had in your head before you started this exercise. If it is drastically lower, go back over the figures and see if there is anything you can trim in a sustainable way. If not, then now may just not be the right time and circumstances to continue with a mortgage application. But so much better to know that now, surely?

Making an Application in Principle

So, now we have our budget figure, we can move onto getting a lending decision by making an Application in Principle.

What is an Application in Principle? To summarise, it is simply an application whereby you tell the lender about your current circumstances, including basic facts like address history, date of birth etc, income, outgoings, and your outline mortgage requirements (covered next). Each lender will require different levels of information at this stage. The lender at this point is taking your word for it – they are not going to ask for proof of anything you say at this stage. However, if the information during a full mortgage application appears to be incorrect the lender can then decline the application so it's important at this stage to be as honest as you can with the information you are supplying. A financial adviser can help you with this.

Many of my clients ask if they should apply for an Application in Principle before they start looking for a house, as it could take them a long time to find one. It is completely your choice – it will trigger a credit check which means this could show on your credit file and affect your current score. So don't feel under pressure to instigate one before you need it. However, until you have an Application in Principle you will have no idea if a lender will in fact lend you money, so you could spend six months looking at houses and not know if you can fund the purchase. Also, if for whatever reason it is declined you can start looking into why it has been declined and take necessary action.

Once you have your Application in Principle and have settled on your budget you can start looking for properties within your price range. Before we start looking into the house-buying process, I will go through your mortgage considerations, needs and objectives, as ideally you should have done this before you apply for an Application in Principle. Why? Well, being clear on what you want out of a mortgage will determine which lender is best for you at the time. One lender may have the cheapest 5-year fixed rate, but another lender may have the cheapest 2-year tracker rate. There is so much to consider when choosing a mortgage and a huge number of factors can affect your choice of most suitable lender, so let's now move onto mortgage consideration, needs and objectives.

Mortgage considerations, needs and objectives

From the outset I have said that this book is more about helping you to buy a house than finding a suitable mortgage. Clearly, as the market is changing all the time, in a book it is not relevant to go into too much detail when it comes to which mortgage products are available. However, I will outline the main types of mortgages that are available, and there is a surprisingly large number of these! I am not making recommendations here – please consult a financial adviser for more detailed advice or investigate each type more for yourself.

When considering a mortgage, start by eliminating mortgage products unsuitable for you. There are thousands of mortgages available at any one time and we are trying to get this down to the one best suited for you. Of course, various mortgages may be broadly suitable, but we want to arrive at the most suitable and cost-effective mortgage for your needs and objectives. To do so, here are the following mortgage considerations, needs and objectives that you need to be aware of.

Repayment type mortgages

There are two main ways in which to repay a mortgage: capital and interest (also known as capital repayment), or interest only.

With a repayment mortgage you pay a certain amount off the mortgage each month over a set term and at the end of the term the mortgage will have been paid off, as long as no payments have been missed and you have kept to the repayment plan. With a capital repayment mortgage, in the early years most of your monthly payment goes towards the interest payment and only a small amount of the capital is paid off. This is because at the start of your term you are paying interest on the full mortgage amount. As time goes by and you have now repaid a larger part of your capital, the interest portion of the monthly payments becomes smaller because the capital you are charged interest on is smaller. The monthly payment remains the same, but you are now paying more and more of the capital, hence the term 'repayment'.

Let's look at a mortgage over the first two years, using the example of a mortgage of £150,000 at an interest rate of 3% over 25 years.

The monthly payment is £711.32p per month but we are going to refer to the annual payment of £8,535.84p

The interest you will pay in the first year will be £4,500 (£150,000 x 3% interest = £4,500)

We then take the interest payment off the annual mortgage payments to find out what we have paid off the mortgage: £8535.84 – £4,500 = £4,035.84

At the start of year two you will owe £145,964.16 (£150,000 – £4,035.84) which means you now pay 3% interest on the lower amount, but your monthly payments stay the same which means more of your payment is now going to capital repayment rather than interest payments compared to the year before and so on, until the end of your mortgage term. Please note that it is unlikely to be quite that straightforward across the 25 years of the mortgage, as the interest rate is likely to vary during that period, but this example gives you an idea of how a capital repayment mortgage works.

Interest-only mortgage

As its name suggests, with an interest-only mortgage you are only paying the interest on the mortgage, **leaving the full mortgage balance to be repaid at the end of the term**. I have put this sentence in bold, as it is vital not to overlook this!! It has been known... To cover this balance commitment, borrowers can take out a long-term investment to use to repay the mortgage at the end of the term. These are usually endowment policies, Individual Savings Accounts (ISAs) or perhaps the tax-free lump sum from a personal pension plan. The value of investments and any income from them can fall as well as rise and you may not get back the original amount invested. We are not going to discuss endowment policies, ISAs or pensions in this book – if you require more information regarding these, please seek advice from a financial adviser.

Some lenders offer an interest-only mortgage without coupling this to an investment repayment vehicle but instead relying on the sale of the mortgaged property at the end of the term. This may suit borrowers looking to downsize when their mortgage term comes to an end.

The monthly payment on an interest-only mortgage, if the interest rate were to remain the same, would not change even if the term was increased or decreased. The only time the monthly payment would change is if the amount of capital altered or the interest rate changed.

Let us look at the other features for both methods:

Capital and interest mortgages
  ~ If payments are not missed, it is guaranteed that the mortgage will be paid off at the end of the term.
  ~ As you are paying off the capital you are more likely to gain equity faster in your property than on interest-only. This will help during any economic downturn when property values may decrease.

~ If moving home in the future a capital and repayment mortgage may give you more of a deposit due to the equity gained.

~ If you were to hit financial difficulties the lender may allow you to make interest-only payments for a period, thus instantly reducing the amount you pay each month.

~ Capital and repayment mortgages can be more flexible, as lenders can extend the term, thereby reducing the monthly payments.

~ They maybe more attractive to elderly clients where the payments on an endowment policy for an interest-only mortgage would be too high.

~ It is strongly advised to take out life cover to protect against the event of death during the term of the mortgage.

Interest-only mortgages

~ When using an endowment, ISA, or cash sum from a personal pension (what is known as the repayment vehicle) there is no guarantee on maturity that there will be sufficient funds to repay the mortgage.

~ Equity in the property is only gained through an increase in the market price for the house.

~ There is no option to reduce the payments if borrowers find themselves in financial difficulty.

~ Interest-only mortgages can be less flexible when considering the term. This will depend on the repayment vehicle. If the repayment vehicle is an endowment policy with a fixed term, the lender may not allow you to extend the mortgage beyond the same term.

~ Endowment policies have life cover built into them which can repay the mortgage in the event of death, but ISAs and personal pension plans have no integral life assurance.

~ There is a possibility the repayment vehicle may provide better returns than assumed when calculating the required premiums/ contribution. In this situation there will be cash available after the capital has been repaid. Over recent years this has become less likely, and more often, borrowers are faced with a shortfall.

~ If joint borrowers were to divorce, an endowment policy can be difficult to unravel. The only way to split the value is to surrender the policy which isn't usually in the policy holders' best interest.

As you can see, there is a great deal to consider, and this is only the start. Another way to look at it is to ask this question: do you want to be safe in the knowledge you will repay the mortgage at the end of the term or are you prepared to take the risk that there could be a shortfall when it comes to repay your mortgage? When faced with that risk, most borrowers nowadays prefer the capital and repayment method of repayment. Of course, this question may be answered for you by the lender's criteria, as interest-only mortgages are not available to everyone.

Term of the mortgage

How long do you want a mortgage for? How do you choose how long you want a mortgage for?

Well, the first issue to look at is what happens when you increase or decrease a mortgage term.

Let us have a starting point of a 25-year term and see what happens if I increase the term. On a capital and repayment mortgage, your monthly payments would reduce, as you now have longer to pay back the capital. However, you will pay more interest over the term of the mortgage as you are now paying the interest for longer. Therefore, the mortgage will cost you more over its total term. Also, be aware that in some circumstances lenders may lend more money based on a longer term too.

If we decrease the term the opposite will happen: your monthly payment will be higher on a capital and repayment mortgage, but you will pay less interest across a shorter term. And a similar principle applies – due to the shorter term the lender may lend less due to the fact that the same income has to be used to repay the same the mortgage but over a shorter period of time.

Now we know the outcome of deciding on a longer or shorter term, what is it in your needs and objectives that is going to decide the term? For example, is it that you want to pay off your mortgage before you retire at state retirement age, or do you want to retire at the age of 50?

Another consideration: do you want to spend a certain amount each month on your mortgage? If so, let's find the term that reflects that.

As each person's circumstances and requirements are different, there is clearly no right or wrong answer to these questions. You just need to ensure that you have discussed all the options and chosen a term that suits your needs and objectives. If you have chosen a 30-year term and you come to the end of your mortgage product of choice, let's say a two-year fixed rate, and on reflection the payments were easily affordable, you could then reduce the term at the point of re-mortgaging. So, although you are committing to a term when you apply for a mortgage, you can change it when your mortgage product comes to an end. A two-year fixed rate will of course come to an end two years after it started, then giving you the opportunity to choose another product, say a five-year fixed rate, so at that point you can change the term if it fits the lender's criteria and affordability.

The mortgage market

The mortgage market is competitive; lenders are always reviewing their range of mortgage products to offer attractive deals to borrowers depending on their circumstances. Due to this there is a wide range of options available, and we need to be sure you are choosing the right one for you. What is more, lenders can change their products at any point they choose to. For example, they may do this if they are lending too much due to being one of the cheapest providers at that time and their funds are running low. Due to this, the lender you may choose today may not be the cheapest even by the time you find the house you want to mortgage. This can be another advantage of using a financial adviser, as they can search for the cheapest product available to them at the time you require the mortgage.

Let us now look at the large array of different options available so that you can make an informed decision when choosing your mortgage product.

Fixed rate mortgages

Fixed rate mortgages, as the name suggests, provide a mortgage fixed rate for a fixed period of time. This is usually two, three, five or even ten years. This fixed rate is not linked to the Bank of England base rate, so if interest rates go up or down your rate of interest will remain the same. This means your monthly payment will not change for the fixed period. This will be a disadvantage if interest rates go down, as your payments will remain the same whereas a borrower on a tracker rate mortgage would see their monthly payments reduce. Turn the scenario around however, and if interest rates increase, you have kept your monthly payments the same whereas the same borrowers on a tracker rate will see an increase in their monthly payments.

It is up to you how long you fix the mortgage for, but the shorter the fixed period the more flexibility you have in regard to changing the mortgage. For example, if you feel that your monthly payments are easily affordable over a term of 30 years, after your 2-year deal has come to an end you can choose to reduce the term to 20 years if it still fits affordability and criteria. If you have chosen a 5-year fixed rate you now need to wait until the end of the 5-year fixed period before you can made any changes to the term, that is if you want to avoid any early repayment charges.

Early repayment charges? Yes, what you need to bear in mind with a fixed rate mortgage is that there will most likely be an early repayment charge if you choose to repay all of the mortgage within the fixed rate period. This is important, as usually the longer you fix the rate for, the higher the early repayment charge.

With this in mind, you must think carefully about your circumstances and objectives, for example, how long you plan to live in the house for. Is this property just a step to the next bigger house when you know you may be able to afford more? If so, what are your timescales? If you plan to move within 2-3 years, it clearly does not make sense to choose a 5-year product.

Having said that, most lenders (but not all) provide the option to port your mortgage. This means that if you are on a fixed rate mortgage but want to move, you can transfer the mortgage to another property. However, if additional funds are required you would need to borrow these from the same lender on a current mortgage product available. The downside is that, to avoid early repayment charges, you would need to stick with your current mortgage provider and their rates may not be favourable, or not secure the funds against the onward purchase property if it doesn't meet their criteria.

Another factor to consider: I have seen a number of first-time buyers, after living with their partner for 6 months, decide they no longer want to continue the relationship. In these unfortunate circumstances, a 2-year fixed rate may have better suited their needs, allowing them to redeem the mortgage and move on with their lives rather than being locked into, say, a 5-year fixed rate. Of course, we do not plan for this to happen but knowing there are options which give you flexibility if they do will help you make a better decision when choosing your mortgage product.

Normally, 2-year fixed rate products tend to have a lower rate of interest than longer fixed terms but don't always take that for granted. If you are unsure whether to fix for a short or a long period take a look at both, to see the difference in cost. Although a 2-year fixed rate might be cheaper today, remember in 2 years you will need to re-mortgage if you want to avoid going onto the lender's variable rate, which of course is usually higher than the fixed rate. There is no certainty with the future trend of interest rates! This makes decisions on the length of fixed-rate commitment a careful choice you need to make.

The key benefit of a fixed rate mortgage is that it offers stability – you know exactly how much your mortgage will be each month for a set period of time, allowing you to better plan your finances and monthly budget.

After the fixed rate period you would either go onto the lender's variable rate or re-mortgage. If re-mortgaging, consider if your circumstances have changed – if you have reduced your hours of work or taken out a loan, is your mortgage still affordable, based on your current circumstances?

Capped and/or collared mortgage

Capped mortgages are guaranteed not to rise above a certain rate of interest for a fixed period. They can also be collared, meaning they will not fall below a certain rate of interest. The rate usually matches the lender's variable rate but offers the safety that your rate of interest will not continue to rise above a certain level even if the lender's variable rate does so.

A capped mortgage could be seen as a better option to a fixed rate, as you have the security of knowing your rate of interest will not go above a certain fixed level but could benefit from a rate reduction.

However, we are seeing fewer collared mortgages being made available, and be aware that early repayment charges may apply to a collared mortgage.

Standard variable rate mortgages

With a standard variable rate mortgage, the rate of interest charged varies throughout the life of the mortgage. The lender will review and set their own standard variable rate based on certain factors:

~ Competitors' rates will influence lenders' decision to increase or decrease standard variable rates
~ The Bank of England's base rate. The Monetary Policy Committee (MPC) meets regularly and sets the Bank of England base rate. However, some lenders do not follow exactly an MPC base rate change when it is announced. If the base rate has increased but the lender's flow of deposits from savers is favourable, the lender may hold off increasing their standard variable rate for a few weeks or even months. And then, even when they do increase their standard variable rate, they may not increase by the full amount of the change to the Bank of England's base rate.

~ The lender may be raising funds themselves for future borrowers and if the cost of lending has increased, they may need to increase their standard variable rate to fund this new finance.

The standard variable rate mortgage can be regarded as the standard type of mortgage, with all other products a variation of it. When your fixed rate mortgage comes to an end it will revert to the standard variable rate. As discussed, the standard variable is likely to be higher than a fixed rate and will be more unpredictable, as the variable rate fluctuates, depending on the Bank of England's rate movements and lenders' financial circumstances.

One advantage with the standard variable rate is that there are less likely to be early repayment charges. This provides the flexibility to repay a mortgage at any time without a penalty, or to re-mortgage and not incur any penalties.

Discounted mortgages

A discounted mortgage is a version of a standard variable rate mortgage. As the title suggests, the rate has been set a certain percentage below (or discounted below) the standard variable rate. For example, if the standard variable rate is 5.74% and you have a discount of 3.5% your interest rate will be 2.24%. If the standard variable rate increases so will your discounted rate. The discount will last for a set period, usually 2 years. After the fixed period you will revert to the standard variable rate, so in this example if there were no increases this would be 5.74%.

Cashback mortgages

Cashback mortgages are offered as an incentive to new borrowers. The lender will offer a certain percentage of the mortgage amount as cash back, usually between 2-6% or a set amount ranging from £250-£1000.

Cashback mortgages are really just a mortgage feature rather than a separate mortgage product, as cashback can be offered on fixed rate mortgages and on variable rate mortgages, depending on the lender's product portfolio and selling objectives at the time.

Be aware with cashback that the mortgage may have a slightly higher interest rate than a product without cashback, so you will need to decide whether you want a lower monthly payment or a slightly higher interest rate. Cashback can help towards those initial overheads of buying a house such as solicitor's fees. Evaluate the true value of any cashback by totalling ALL costs (monthly mortgage payments, any arrangement fees, and exit fees) for the comparable versions with and without cashback, and see whether in fact, you do end up with cash back! The FCA advises not using cashback to influence your decision, as within the context of the term of a mortgage and the sums involved, it is always going to represent a small percentage, but it is a feature you can consider.

Tracker rate mortgages

Tracker rate mortgages are variable rate mortgages that have an automatic link built so that its interest rate 'tracks' an index, usually the Bank of England's base rate or the London Interbank Offered Rate (LIBOR), which is the rate banks lend to each other. The LIBOR is set by market forces so can be more volatile than the Bank of England's base rate.

If interest rates go down your mortgage payment will go down and if interest rates go up your monthly payment will go up.

The MPC (Monetary Policy Committee) decide on any changes to the Bank of England's base rate 8 times a year. If you believe strongly that interest rates are likely to fluctuate you may want to consider a tracker rate. Your monthly payments will then potentially be subject to significant fluctuations at short notice. If you are not comfortable with that, then you may prefer to consider a fixed rate mortgage.

Offset mortgages/Current account mortgages

An offset mortgage is an arrangement where the borrower has their mortgage account, savings account, and current account with the same provider. Any positive balances in the savings account and current account are offset against the negative mortgage account. So, if your mortgage is £150,000 and you have savings of £50,000 you will only pay interest on £100,000. If you keep your mortgage payments the same you will overpay your mortgage, reducing the term, saving you money on interest payments.

Current account mortgages are similar, although only one account, a current account, is linked. This will be the current account the borrower's salary and savings are paid into and where the mortgage is debited. In other words, it is a current account with a huge overdraft facility, but the interest rates are more on par with mortgage rates. Any surplus of income over outgoings in a month is used to reduce the mortgage loan.

Any overpayment with both mortgages is accessible if needed but if you choose not to overpay, your mortgage will decrease at the same term set out at the start of the mortgage.

Shared ownership mortgage

A shared ownership mortgage allows a borrower to buy a stake in a property, usually 25-50% of the value of the property. The remainder of the property is often owned by a housing association. Housing associations are not-for-profit organisations who provide affordable housing to buy, rent or both (shared ownership). The borrower will take out a mortgage for the percentage they wish to buy. You will still most likely need to put a deposit down for your share of the property. For example, if you were buying a 50% share in a property worth £150,000 you would need to raise £75,000 worth of funds to buy your half. If you were to put down a 10%

deposit you would require £7,500 for your deposit meaning your mortgage would be for £69,500.

When you buy a shared ownership property, you will pay your mortgage payments and a rent payment to the landlord (most likely a housing association). If the property is sold you will be entitled to the capital raised on your portion of the property.

With shared ownership mortgages you have a degree of flexibility, as you can choose to purchase more shares in the property. For example, you can increase your share from 25% to 50% then to 75% and even purchase 100% of the property if you wish to. This is known as 'staircasing'.

Home purchase plans – Islamic mortgages

According to the FCA, "A home purchase plan serves the same purpose as a regular mortgage – it provides consumers with the finances for buying a home – but it is structured in a way that makes it acceptable under Islamic law. As interest is contrary to Islamic law, a home purchase plan is in essence a sale and lease arrangement."

With a home purchase plan, the bank, building society or other provider offering the plan will buy the property and become the legal owner. At the end of a fixed period there is an arrangement for you to buy the property for the purchase price originally paid by the bank. You can choose to sell before then if you wish too.

Since the lender owns the property, you will take out a lease to rent the property from them.

This means your monthly payments will be a combination of rent and of money going towards buying out the lender's stake in the property. No interest is payable.

Provided you keep to the payments agreed in the terms, at the end of the term you will have bought out the lender and be sole owner of the property.

There are two forms of Sharia-compliant home purchase plans: Ijara and Diminishing Musharaka

~ Ijara is a term referring to the leasing element of a home purchase plan. With an Ijara plan the monthly payments you make are part rent and part capital, and there will be charges also included in your payment. The bank or building society keep your capital saved until the end of the term, at which point your capital is used to purchase the property. This means that throughout the term of the agreement your share in the property remains the same until the lender's stake is bought out.

~ Diminishing Musharaka is essentially a co-ownership agreement. This means both you and the lender own the property together, with separate stakes. Each payment you make is part rent and part capital, used to purchase the lender's shares in the property. There will also be charges included in your payment. As your stake increases the lender's decreases. Because of this the rent you pay also reduces as the lender then owns less of the property.

Lifetime mortgages and home reversion plans

Lifetime mortgages are like shared ownership although there are two main differences:

~ They are only available to older buyers, normally over 55.
~ There is no final redemption date. This means it is captured by the FCA's definition of a regulated lifetime mortgage contract.

Home reversion plans are similar to lifetime mortgages, but they also allow a homeowner to release equity from a property. This is achieved by selling the property or a percentage of the property to the home reversion plan provider. The sale price is usually significantly lower than the true value of the property but can allow the borrower to raise more money than through a lifetime mortgage.

You will need to take legal advice before releasing equity from your home as Lifetime Mortgages and Home Reversion plans are not right for everyone. Not all mortgage advisers offer Lifetime mortgages and they may refer you to a specialist.

Mortgage fees

Lenders have multiple products which have multiple features. One way a lender can make their product stand out and be more attractive is by offering a lower rate of interest for a fee, known as an arrangement fee. This is not to be mistaken for the valuation fee.

The arrangement fee is a fee charged by the lender and in return they offer a lower interest rate, thus lowering your monthly payments. They may also offer a product without a fee but a slightly higher interest rate, meaning your monthly payments are higher.

There will be an option to add this fee to the loan if it fits in with affordability. However, if you do this you need to consider that you will then pay interest on that fee for the term of the mortgage.

As with cashback, it is always best to look at both options and see actually what you will pay over the term of that product, taking into account all payments and charges. By adding an arrangement fee to the mortgage or by choosing a mortgage without such a fee, you will reduce your upfront costs during the application process, particularly at a time when you will have various other fees to pay – solicitor's fees, removal and estate agency costs, plus potentially many other calls on your cash.

A valuation fee is the fee payable to the lender for them to arrive at an accurate current valuation of the property you are purchasing, for the purposes of the mortgage. This is rarely exactly the same as the price you are paying for the property! This then is different from an arrangement fee and, in most circumstances, cannot be added to the mortgage. This is because the lender is usually paying an external company to complete the valuation survey. We will discuss different types of survey later.

Not all lenders charge a valuation fee, as this is another feature that can make a mortgage product attractive to a potential borrower.

Finding a home

Now we have our budget, and we know our available purchase price, we can start getting excited about looking for a house. Details of properties being sold can be found from selling agents, estate agents or property marketing websites such as Rightmove and Zoopla, or now more rarely, in local newspapers.

You are now the potential purchaser, and any purchaser should consider some or all the following points:

~ What size property do you need? How many bedrooms? How much parking and garden do you require? Do you want to be detached or linked to your neighbour? Is an apartment more suited to your needs? How old is the property? Do you want a new-build? Does it have gas or electric or both? How energy efficient is it? How much is the Council Tax?

~ How close is the house to your work? Not only this, what are the transport links like to get to work? We all know that some roads seem to be gridlocked at certain times of the day, so check out the roads, say, at rush hour and at school times. It's worth the research now rather than on the first day in your new home.

~ How close are the schools? And what is the OFSTED report for those schools? When my wife and I bought our house, we did not have children, so I did not even think about this but then found ourselves out of the catchment area for the school my wife and I wanted our children to go to. We were lucky and secured the school we chose even though there is a closer school nearby, but this is something you should consider if you do or even if you do not have children. School catchment can have a significant bearing on the price of the house.

~ Consider road links, public transport, cycle routes and the logistics to reaching relatives and friends. You may need to be close to a motorway as you travel for work, or you may need to get a train to an airport. Family, especially grandparents, are becoming more relied upon for childcare, so can they get to your home easily and at a reasonable time or is it going to add another hour to your journey to pick them up after work. Do your relatives need care and how often?

~ Is it located in an urban or rural area? Do you like to nip into a coffee shop and catchup with your social media or friends? Do you like being left alone in the middle of nowhere or do you like both? It's essential to visit the area you are considering buying to "get a feel for it". If you are looking at multiple properties make a day of it, visit a coffee shop in the area and have a look around the shops. Doing this also helps you get to know the selling agents in the area and what type and size of property is selling for what price. It's also nice to put a face to a name if you have been dealing with an agent on the phone or on the internet.

~ These questions are just part of what you should be asking yourselves. Proximity to a good gym may be essential to one person and irrelevant to another, likewise, for example, ease of access to a doctor's, a vet, a nursery, a pharmacist, a pub... the list goes on. As each person or family's requirements are unique, draw up a list with three columns, one titled 'Must have', the second 'Nice to have' and the third, 'Don't need'. Then, for each property on your shortlist, see which most closely match your criteria. On the next page is a form you can use.

Your requirements for your ideal house

MUST HAVE	NICE TO HAVE	DON'T NEED

Role of the seller

As the purchaser, you will be buying off the seller, or vendor as they are referred to, so what is their responsibility in all this?

~ In bringing the property to market, first they must decide that they really want to move and sell their home. There are vendors who put their house up for sale simply to "test the waters", and if they don't get the price they want, simply don't sell, which can be annoying. However, most vendors have made the decision that they want to find a new house themselves and need to sell their current property to move on. It's always worth asking the question of the vendor, "Why are you moving?" It's a question that purchasers worry about asking, but I always want to know why to make sure it's not a reason that would put me off buying the house. There is most likely a perfectly good reason, like they have outgrown the property or even need to downsize. I once asked this question when viewing a property and the vendor became very uncomfortable and I didn't really get a straight answer. I don't know if I made the guy nervous or if he was hiding something, but if I was moving house, I would normally know the reason why and have no problem explaining it. I may have missed a great house but this put me off so I will never know.

~ Set a sale price: they may do this through an estate agent, which I will discuss later, or they may market the property themselves. Either way a sale price will need to be agreed on when a purchaser negotiates an offer.

~ The vendor needs to agree the items that will be included and excluded in the sale price. They will do this by filling out their solicitor's enquiry form. They won't list every item, but the law distinguishes between fixtures and fittings. Fixtures are assumed to be an integral part of the property such as kitchen cupboards, fitted wardrobes and fitted carpets.

~ Fittings are household items or appliances that can be taken away by the seller unless there is an agreement to include them in the sale price. Once the vendor has agreed to leave those said fittings, they are obliged to fulfil this part of the transaction. Any doubt can be resolved with the acting solicitors for both parties.

~ They must give truthful answers to any enquiries made by the purchaser or their legal representative. This includes the noisy neighbour if questioned about it. This leads back to my question, "Why are you moving"? You can also ask if there are any complaints or disputes with neighbours and the vendor is legally obliged to answer truthfully.

~ The vendor must vacate the property and give up the property on the date of entry. This might sound silly or obvious but there are cases where the vendor's onward purchase may not have completed, or their future rented accommodation is not ready, and they try to stay in their current property. Therefore, solicitors usually organise a whole property chain to move on the same day to avoid this happening. The property chain is where homebuyers and sellers are linked, as their onward purchase or sale depends on a transaction with someone else in the chain. First-time buyers can be seen as more favourable as they are not dependent on any chain because they have no property to sell.

~ It is the vendor who traditionally remunerates the estate agent, which is why as the purchaser you do not have any estate agency costs (unless you are selling too of course). However, there are some new estate agents trying to do things different whereby it is the buyer who pays rather than the vendor. This is to attract more vendors to that estate agency, so it is best to check either way.

When a seller accepts an offer in England, Wales or Northern Ireland, the offer is "subject to contract" which you may see on the estate agents' websites or in newspapers. This means the vendor is not bound until the contracts are exchanged and that the agreement on price is provisional. I make this point, as during the survey or legal process certain factors may arise such as a lowering of a valuation, when the surveyor believes the house is worth less than you are paying for it. In this case you may want to renegotiate the price. This can also lead to the practices of 'gazumping', 'gazundering', and even 'gazanging' – no, I have not taken these from a Roald Dahl book.

Gazumping starts to occur when property prices are rising. The vendor may have already accepted an offer but then accepts a higher offer from another purchaser before contracts have been exchanged. The original purchaser loses out on the property and may have already incurred considerable costs, such as a survey, which will now lead to nothing and have no means of recompense.

Gazundering happens usually when house prices are falling. They buyer waits until contracts are about to be exchanged and then lowers the offer on the property. The vendor then may be worried they may struggle to find another buyer and if there has been a property chain going on for some time, the vendor may feel forced to accept this lower offer to complete their transaction so they can also move on to their next property.

Gazanging is when a vendor pulls out of a property transaction even though an offer has been accepted. Again, as contracts have not exchanged the vendor is allowed to do this. This can happen due to the vendor simply getting "cold feet" or simply the vendor cannot find a more suitable house to move too. There can be understandable circumstances in which this can occur, but with gazumping and gazundering... well, I hope you can still sleep well at night if you indulge in this!

You can now see why it is important to exchange contracts quickly, as once contracts are exchanged if the vendor pulls out you can take legal action to try to recoup the money you have spent. A financial adviser may be able to ease the application process and liaise with estate agents and solicitor to ensure a smooth and swift exchange of contracts and therefore avoid these situations. So, ask your financial adviser exactly what they will help you with during the purchase process when choosing which one to use.

As a purchaser you may also need to sell and may be thinking of using an estate agent to do this. Depending on the estate agent, the services they offer may vary, but many offer a comprehensive service include property listing, surveys, valuation services, mortgage and insurance advice, as well as property rental services.

Role of estate agents

The estate agent ultimately represents the seller/vendor. Although I'm sure they will also try and offer the best service to the purchaser they do not represent the purchaser.

Estate agents make their money from commission, which is usually a percentage of the sale price of the property they have sold, although some may charge a flat fee. The vendor will pay this. The estate agents may also offer a discounted rate if you solely sell through them and do not use multiple agents to sell your property.

The estate agents can help you set an optimum sell price, as they will be selling other houses in the area and may have sold houses recently in the area which are similar to yours. They will have a clear picture as to what you can expect to achieve as the sale price for your property.

There are two ways to bring a property to market, which are private treaty and public auction:

~ Private treaty is the most common and is the formal term for the way estate agents market the property and organise appointments for potential purchasers to view it. They negotiate a formal offer which is agreed subject to contract and then the necessary legal work can commence.

~ Public auction is not as popular as private treaty but can be appropriate for certain types of property or circumstances. Examples would be the property being in poor condition and therefore unfit for mortgage lending; the property is being sold by executors when disposing of assets from a deceased persons estate; or the property may have been repossessed and the lender wants a quick sale to recoup their funds.

~ If you've ever watched *Homes Under the Hammer*, you will know what a sale by auction entails. It requires careful consideration, and you must decide on a minimum price you are happy to receive. You can then set a reserve so that if no one offers more than this figure you won't have to sell the property, but you may incur auctioneer's costs. There are also risks with selling your property at auction such as the bidder's offer falling through. Technically a bid is legally accepted, and the seller can sue if the bidder cannot follow through with the purchase, but this costs time and money. There is a great deal to consider when selling your house at auction and I would advise if you are seriously considering selling at auction to speak with an estate agent or an auction house to find out more.

The estate agent will promote the sale of the property usually through advertising in newspapers, property marketing websites, their own website, and their shop windows. The advertisement will usually show you a picture of the property, and give a brief description which may include:

type of property ie detached house or bungalow, semi-
detached house, apartment etc

scope of the accommodation – how many bedrooms, toilets, and
bathrooms etc

~ Size of the plot

~ Location of the property

~ Tenure – either freehold, leasehold or commonhold. Freehold
is where you own the property and the land it is built on and
have responsibility to maintain both the property and the land.
Leasehold gives the right to a person to occupy the land for a
specified period and ground rent is charged to the occupier. When
you buy a house or flat which is leasehold, the lease is transferred
from the seller's name to yours. You need to consider how much
the ground rent will be and if there is a service charge to maintain
the land and ensure you have factored this into your affordability
for a mortgage. You also need to find out the terms of the ground
rent and service charge, as there have been cases where ground
rent and service charges have increased substantially every 5
– 10 years. This should be stated in the lease or service charge
contract. Also, you must find out how many years are left on the
lease. Leases can start from 99 years to 999 years but if you are
buying a home which is not a new build, the lease may have a
short term left to run, which will need to fit the lender's criteria.
Anything below 80 years and I would check their criteria.

~ Commonhold is where owners of an apartment block can form
a commonhold association to assert their joint rights over their
respective properties. The commonhold association owns the
land, the building, and the common areas, but the flat owners
own each individual flat. Unlike leasehold there is no term, so the
rights of the flat owners within the commonhold association is
never-ending.

The estate agents will advertise the property at a price agreed with the
seller and invite offers around this price. They can also invite 'closed
bids' whereby a purchaser will write a letter with the maximum they are
prepared to offer and an explanation as to why they should be chosen by
the vendor to buy. The vendor can then accept either the highest bid or the
purchaser who is in the best position to proceed. Not all vendors choose

simply the highest price. They may have found a property and want to move before they get gazumped and if you are in a position to be the quickest to complete the purchase, your offer may win out, so bear this in mind when making your offers.

The estate agents' work is not complete until there is an exchange of contracts, so the estate agents will monitor the progress of the sale through the solicitors acting for each party.

Types of property

Residential properties come in all shapes and sizes. You can have detached properties, semi-detached properties, bungalows, 3-storey town houses, terraced houses, the list goes on. What is important about the property you want to buy is that it is mortgageable or a surveyor deems it fit for mortgage purposes. We will now look at some factors which may affect an application during a survey, which you may want to enquire about during your initial viewings.

Location, location, location

As that well-known property programme title underlines, it is the location of a property which is the factor which has the greatest effect on the value of a property. For example, a 3-bedroom detached house in London will be worth far more than the equivalent property in Bradford. An apartment in an affluent town will be worth more than an apartment 1 mile away surrounded by social housing. In a worst-case scenario, a lender may feel that the location is so poor that there is a chance the property will not be suitable for resale if they were to repossess and so decline the mortgage application based on the property's location even though your circumstances are suitable for lending.

What is it built from?

Most houses in the UK are built from brick and block and have a tile or slate roof. This would be classed as standard construction, but of course not all houses are built the same. Some houses have less durable materials such as thatched roofs or flat roofs with a felt covering. Some houses were built using concrete and depending on the builder and concrete type used this may result in an unsuccessful application.

My advice is simply to ask the question, "Is it a standard construction?" You may think this is obvious from looking from the outside, but some local authority houses were built out of concrete with then a brick veneer applied to the outside, making it look like a standard construction, or it may be that it was rendered and painted.

A property may be in a conservation/heritage area and may have strict restrictions on the materials which can be used to build and repair them. The important question here is if you see work has been done on the property to make sure it has been completed to the correct restrictions, as you could find yourself responsible for returning the property to its original state, a costly proposition.

Age of the property

The age of the property won't affect the price too much, but very old properties can be expensive to maintain. Also, with old properties there may be planning permission restrictions. I point this out as some older houses tend to have large gardens and potential buyers think they can extend out in the future only to find out they cannot due to these restrictions.

A new-build property might be seen as a sure win for a lender, but they still can decline an application if not satisfied with a builder's guarantee. An example of a reputable guarantee is the National House Building Councils (NHBC) Guarantee but there are other providers, especially for smaller developments. It is always best to ask what guarantee scheme has been used and liaise with your mortgage lender or financial adviser to check if this will be OK.

Use of the property

Most houses are for residential use, but some have both a residential and a commercial use. An example of this is a newsagents where the owner lives in the flat above the shop. Most lenders will require at least 40% of the property to be for residential use to lend on but it is always worth discussing with your lender or financial adviser before making an offer to make sure they will be OK with it.

Applying for the mortgage

We are now at the point in our journey where you have chosen your property and made an offer on it. You have provided your application in principle, a proof of deposit, and the name of your solicitor.

Once you have had your offer accepted you can start the mortgage application process and instruct your solicitor. In this chapter we will describe the mortgage application process, and in the next chapter we will go through the conveyancing process. I have done it that way around on purpose, as some buyers prefer to wait until they have had their mortgage offer before they start paying for solicitors just in case it falls through for some reason, such as the property being down valued or the surveyor finding faults with the property.

If going direct to the bank you will need to organise an appointment either face-to-face or over the phone. It can be difficult sometimes getting an appointment at short notice with a bank which is why having a financial adviser can speed up the process. All lenders have different policies so will require different documentation and evidence, so check what they will require before you go.

If using a financial adviser let them know your offer has been accepted and they will then start to organise the mortgage application. Your adviser will most likely require proof of income. If you are employed this means providing payslips; if self-employed, your accounts, SA302s, tax year overviews and an accountant's reference. Also provide bank statements showing your income going into the bank.

If you earn bonuses, commission, or receive benefits you will also need to evidence this income.

You will need to provide photo ID and possibly address ID.

Depending on your circumstances, you may be asked for more documents than I have listed, such as a gifted deposit letter if you are receiving a gift from someone (usually a family member) for your deposit. The list of documents required will depend on your lender's requirements, but your mortgage adviser will know what is required and advise you appropriately.

Along with these documents you will need details of the property:

~ Address
~ Property description ie detached, bungalow, flat
~ Number of bedrooms
~ Number of bathrooms
~ Number of garages, parking spaces or how many cars fit on the drive
~ Year property was built
~ Land ownership (is it freehold, leasehold or commonhold)

You will need the bank account details you want the monthly mortgage payments to be paid from, details of the estate agents you are buying the property through and your solicitor's details.

Before your mortgage adviser or bank apply for your mortgage, they should read through the illustration document which breaks down the detail of the mortgage and the costs to you, such as mortgage product fees, and broker (adviser) fees. It will also list the commission received by your mortgage adviser from the lender for placing your mortgage with them.

Your mortgage adviser can now submit the full mortgage application and send off the evidence requested from the lender.

Once this has been done your application will be allocated to an underwriter and a valuation will be organised by the lender. Some lenders organise the valuation straightaway while some wait until your documents have been assessed and approved.

Property valuation report (survey)

We are now going to look at the different types and purpose of the valuation report. You will need to decide which type of report you require on your full mortgage application, so it is best to know now what each of them entails.

The three types of valuation reports or survey are:

1. Basic valuation or mortgage valuation
2. Homebuyer's survey and valuation report
3. Full building survey

With mortgage lending, the money which is borrowed from the lender is secured against the property it is used to buy. This means that if you fail to repay the mortgage the lender can use the sale of the property to repay the mortgage. Because the lenders are using the property for security they of course need to know if it is worth enough money to repay the mortgage. Now, there are two things to consider here when the lender receives the valuation report:

1. Is the property worth more than the mortgage amount, and if they were to repossess the property to sell, would the sale pay back the mortgage?
2. Has the valuation affected the loan to value of the mortgage? For example, if you are buying for £200,000 and have a 10% deposit (£20,000) you will have a 90% loan to value mortgage product and the bank will be willing to lend you £180,000 based on this loan to value (assuming affordability fits).

3. If the property is down-valued to £190,000, based on the loan to value the lender may now only be prepared to lend you £171,000 (90% of £190,000).

The lender will only require a **basic valuation report** to achieve their aim, but we will look at the nature of all three reports.

Basic valuation report or mortgage valuation

The basic valuation or mortgage valuation is a superficial inspection of the property for the lender's benefit, even though you may have been charged the valuation fee if there is one.

It simply provides an open market value of the property on which the maximum mortgage amount is based upon.

It will also include an insurance value for the purposes of your building's insurance. The insurance value maybe higher or lower than the market value. The surveyor is estimating the cost to rebuild the property, and the materials used and style of the property will influence this build cost. Also, if the property is linked to another property, they may consider any damage caused to it in the event of partial destruction or collapse.

The report may also include the most obvious defects. This may include a recommendation of repairs needed to the property which could need completing before an offer is issued. If that happens, the mortgage could be subject to a retention equalling the cost of repairs meaning you won't receive the full mortgage offer.

Of course, all this is subject to the fact that a surveyor actually visits the property. Lenders are now moving towards automated valuation which are completed from the surveyor's desktop.

What is important for you to know with this report is that the valuer invariably disclaims any responsibility for the purchase price being reasonable and for the condition of the property. These disclaimers will also be in your mortgage offer document or on the initial application, so the onus is on the buyer to satisfy themselves as to the value of the property they intend to purchase.

Here is an example of what you may see on a basic valuation report:

The Valuer's Report		
Terms and conditions of engagement	A full copy of terms and conditions may be appended to the report submitted to the lender or purchaser stating the scope and any limitations of the service to be provided.	
Names of Clients		
Address of property		
Situation and description	1	Type of property (house, bungalow, flat, etc)
	2	Date (or approximate date) of construction
	3	Method of construction, eg 'main walls cavity brickwork, part rendered, roof pitches and tiles'
	4	General repair and condition
	5	Services, eg mains gas, water, electricity, and drainage
	6	Accommodation – the number of bedrooms, sometimes listed by category (receptions, bedrooms, etc.)
Recommendations	1	Confirmation as to whether the property is suitable for mortgage purposes
	2	Value for mortgage purposes
	3	Reinstatement value for insurance purposes
Essential works that must be carried out	These can be prior to formal offer, subject to undertaking or subject to retention	
Valuer's signature and date		
Standard disclaimers that the valuation is for mortgage purposes only and provides no warranty as to the condition of the property or the reasonableness of the purchase price.		

Ref: – Table taken from CII Mortgage Advice CF6

Homebuyer's Report and Valuation Report

Despite the limited scope of a basic valuation most purchasers do rely on them as the single source of information dictating the condition of the property. This may be down to a lack of understanding of what is involved in the basic report or down to cost. Buying a house involves many different costs and choosing a basic valuation report can reduce these.

During the late 1970s lenders started to look at ways of providing a new added value service which might encourage purchasers to commission a more detailed report on the property they were considering buying. This resulted in the introduction of Homebuyer's Reports by the RICS (Royal Institute of Chartered Surveyors) and ISVA (Independent Surveyors and Valuers Association). Please note: the ISVA no longer exists.

These reports are not comprehensive, but they are likely to highlight the more prominent defects that exist in the property at the time of inspection. However, please bear in mind that there is very little comeback on the shortcomings of a Homebuyers Report, but how the survey is conducted is at least more consistent in relation to the importance of the purchase, in the sense you can be assured a surveyor will take a more in-depth look at the property you are potentially about to commit hundreds of thousands of pounds to and potentially 25 years or more of your life.

The report will find out if there are any structural problems, such as subsidence or damp, as well as any other hidden issues inside or outside the house.

The report doesn't look beyond the floorboards or behind the walls, and any possible repairs that might need to be conducted in the property will be given an estimated cost of repair, such as the house may need the electrics rewiring and the estimate is £3,000.

You can then use this figure to renegotiate the purchase price of the property, or ask the vendors to complete the works, or pull out of the purchase if you feel the cost and disruption of the works is too much.

Most Homebuyer's Reports don't come with a valuation, so you may need to ask this to be added on to the survey, so always check when requesting quotes that they will also provide a valuation. The typical cost for a Homebuyer's Report starts from around £400. If you are using the lender's surveyors, they normally provide a valuation as this is the most important information to the lender.

RICS (Royal Institution of Chartered Surveyors) also provide a Condition Report. The RICS Condition Report should be used for a conventional house, flats or bungalows built from common building materials and in reasonable condition.

It focuses purely on the condition of the property by setting out the following:

- Clear 'traffic light' ratings of the condition of different parts of the building, services, garage, and outbuildings, showing problems that may require varying degrees of attention.
- A summary of the risks to the condition of the building.
- Advice on replacement parts guarantees, planning and control matters for your legal advisers.

The RICS Condition Report does not include a valuation.

Full Building Survey

The Full Building Survey is a comprehensive report on all salient aspects of the property. It provides complete peace of mind, and you can be confident that defects will be identified and reported on. The cost of a Full Building Survey is based on a sliding scale according to the size or value of the property to be inspected. They are more expensive than the other reports which is why most purchasers are not prepared to pay for the report at a time when they are incurring high expenditure to buy the property. A starting cost would be around £500 upwards.

The report is suitable for all residential properties and is particularly good if you are buying an older property or one that might need repairs. Although the survey does not look under floorboards or behind walls it should include the surveyor's opinion on any potential hidden defects.

Like the Homebuyer's Report, the surveyor should also give estimates of the potential cost of repairs.

The Full Building Survey usually doesn't include a valuation so if this is something you require, please make sure you request this.

Underwriting

The mortgage application is usually accepted at application, but the underwriter will need to complete a few checks before issuing the mortgage offer.

The role of the underwriter is mostly risk management but increasingly is required to manage compliance too.

What an underwriter will be asking themselves is, can the applicant service this mortgage based on the information and evidence provided? Also, is the information and evidence provided correct?

Lenders will have a robust underwriting policy in place especially in regard to checking the plausibility of information submitted by the applicant and third parties.

As I have already mentioned, all lenders will have their own lending policy and the underwriter will need to ensure the application complies with this. Where one application may fail with one lender, it could go through with another based on their difference in lending policy or criteria.

Following these checks there are three possible outcomes:

1. Confirmation that the mortgage can move forward, and an offer given, subject to valuation
2. More information or documents may be required
3. The application could be declined

Your mortgage adviser will guide you through each outcome. If more information or documents are required, they will request them from you and submit them along with the original documents. They may already have the information and therefore may not need to contact you.

If your application is declined, they will be able to look for other potential lenders.

If you have gone direct to the lender, they will be able to request more information from you but if the application declines, they will not be able to look for other lenders and you will have to start the process again of finding another lender.

Mortgage offer

So, we have now got a mortgage offer and things are looking positive and secure. However, the offer does not bind the lender as a contractual commitment to lend and is always made conditionally. It should be regarded as an expression of a willingness to enter into a contract with you, the borrower, subject to specific conditions being met.

The mortgage offer is a document usually received in the post, but more lenders are opting into e-documents and emailing mortgage offers to applicants. The offer always includes:

~ Standard conditions that are applicable to all mortgages; and
~ Special conditions applicable to that individual application

There are certain circumstances where the lender may withdraw their offer. This could arise because:

~ After the issue of offer, new information becomes available that changes the nature of the risk, such as the borrower losing their job or taking lower-paid employment.
~ It is found that some of the information provided at offer stage is untrue or cannot be verified by appropriate evidence.
~ The property may have been damaged or destroyed.
~ An intention to defraud the lender is discovered.

Contents of the mortgage offer should set out information on the customer, the property to be mortgaged, details of the mortgage to be provided and any conditions that will apply to the mortgage.

Personal details of applicant(s)	1	Names(s) and current address(es)
	2	Customer number
Property to be mortgaged	1	Address (or, if new, plot number)
	2	Tenure, freehold, leasehold or commonhold (in England)
The mortgage	1	Amount offered and term
	2	Method of repayment
	3	Monthly repayment
	4	Initial rate of interest and the annual percentage rate (some lenders specify APR only)
	5	Characteristics of the rate of interest applicable to the account, such as whether it is a fixed, variable, discounted, stepped, or capped
	6	The period for which any initial interest rate condition will apply and a statement that the rate will revert to standard variable on a specified future date
	7	Cash back and clawback
	8	Fees and charges, including early repayment fees
Standard conditions	1	The lender may withdraw or vary the offer at any time up to completion
	2	The offer will expire after a specified time
	3	The offer is made subject to the property being vacant of any third-party occupants
	4	The offer is made subject to satisfactory investigation of title
	5	The lender accepts no responsibility for the price or value of the property being reasonable
	6	The lender accepts no responsibility for the price or value of the property being reasonable

Specific conditions of offer	1	The offer is made subject to a higher lending charge being paid by the borrower; this may apply to applications for high loan to value mortgages
	2	Undertaking to carry out specified repairs within a specified time
	3	Retention of funds not to be released until specified repairs have been carried out
	4	Staged payments and drawdown intervals (self-build projects)
	5	Completion of access roads
	6	Repayment of other borrowings (this is a common condition when the mortgage is for debt consolidation)
	7	Guarantor contract
	8	Consent to mortgage form – required when a person aged over 17 years will occupy but will not be party to the mortgage; the purpose being to waive any rights of residence by preventing an overriding interest being established under the Land Registration Act 2002

Ref: – Table taken from CII Mortgage Advice CF6

Your mortgage offer will be sent to you, your mortgage adviser, and your conveyancer (solicitor).

We will now look at the role of the legal adviser: solicitors and conveyancers.

Role of the legal adviser: solicitor/ conveyancers

I refer to solicitors as the money handlers, but they are so much more than that. All lenders have a minimum standard which must be met when handling the legal work associated with buying a house before they will consider offering mortgage finance. Until recently it was necessary to use a solicitor, but deregulation in this field has brought about a more competitive environment and some lenders are prepared to allow licenced conveyancing firms to act.

You as the purchaser must find out the lender's requirements in this area. Some lenders, for example, will not permit sole practitioners to act, while others insist on specified minimum safe deposit facilities being in place. Most lenders will have a panel of solicitors which have already been approved and, if using one, your mortgage adviser will be able to check this for you or you can contact the lender yourself. From now on in this chapter, I will use the term solicitor, although most of these functions can also be fulfilled by a licensed conveyancer.

The role of the solicitor is:

- ~ Investigation/examination of title
- ~ Processing and completion of the home purchase transaction and, where applicable, sale of an existing property
- ~ Instructing searches
- ~ Drawing up and execution of the mortgage documentation as required by the lender
- ~ Dealing with all financial aspects of the transactions (both the purchase and the mortgage)
- ~ Advising the purchaser and the lender on relevant issues
- ~ Exchanging contracts/organising completion date

I will now go through these individually.

Investigation of title

Title deeds are legal documents that show who is officially the owner and who holds title to a property or land. Title deeds are sometimes known as land certificates and need to be officially registered with the HM Land Registry. What the solicitor is investigating is simply that the seller is entitled to sell the property and that the property offered is exactly what you believe it to be.

There are factors which can hinder or even prevent a seller from selling the property. For example, where a couple have divorced or separated, resulting in one of the couple wanting to sell and the other not. Another scenario may be that the mortgage on the property being sold may be in one name, but a partner or spouse may have an interest under the Family Law Act 1996 preventing a sale from taking place.

To make things interesting, the property will be either registered or unregistered. The reason for this is land registration, which was introduced with the Land Registration Act 1925. From that point on it became compulsory to register your land and property on purchase. So, if the property you are buying has not been sold since before this time (increasingly unlikely as time goes on) it may be unregistered, and specific processes must be followed to confirm title.

As a rule, investigation of title is carried out by searching:

- ~ The Land Registry – in the case of registered land
- ~ The Land Charges Registry – in the case of unregistered land

Registration confirms matters relating to the property itself, proprietorship (state or right of ownership) and charges or burdens over the land. An example of a charge would be if there is already a mortgage in place when the current owners bought the property to buy the property whereby a mortgage provider will have a charge over the title.

Registration provides a state guarantee that the details registered are correct. Ownership and any rights over the land can therefore be verified by the solicitor without difficulty or risk to the purchaser.

Where the land is unregistered, the solicitor must establish a good 'root of title' by searching back over the history of the property for the last 15 years. The solicitor will also carry out a local land charges search to find out if there are any local plans such as road building or planning permission for industrial businesses due to take place in the surrounding area.

The sale of the property will include most or all fixtures, but it is important for you to find out what fittings or movable items are included in the purchase price. This is usually done by requesting that the sellers complete a form specifying exactly what is and is not included in the purchase price. This will be done through the two solicitors acting on behalf of the buyer and the vendor and will form the basis of the contract between the parties.

Processing and completion of the home purchase transaction and, where applicable, sale of an existing property.

When you make an offer to purchase a property this is usually 'subject to contract' which means the prospective purchaser can withdraw from the transaction at any time until a legal contract is executed. This is known as private treaty and constitutes the agreement for the sale of a property at a price negotiated directly between the vendor and purchaser or their agents.

In some cases, the solicitor acting for the vendor can request a deposit of 10% from the purchaser. This acts as a stake-holding, as well as an indication of good faith. However, in recent times, as deposits have become smaller and lending loan to values have increased, these upfront deposits have been waivered or are not necessary at all and are now paid on exchange.

The solicitors acting for the vendor and the solicitors acting for the buyer draw up contracts for the sale and purchase. The contracts commit the buyer and the vendor to complete the transaction when exchanged. Before exchange is permitted, the solicitor for the purchaser will:

~ Ensure there is good title
~ Ensure that sufficient funds are in place to complete the transaction
~ Ensure that other factors, such as the sale of an existing property, or bridging finance pending sale, are in order

It is normal to draft contracts early but to leave the completion date open until it is certain that the transaction can be concluded by that date.

When you exchange contracts, you are going to need buildings insurance in place, as you are now committed to buy. Should any problems arise on the property that are not covered on the vendor's policy, you will still have to go ahead with the purchase on the terms originally agreed.

When contracts are exchanged, the vendor is committed to sell and the purchaser is committed to buy. Exchange of contracts is therefore the 'point of no return'. Failure to complete by the specified date can result in daily penalty interest being payable. The person being prevented from completion may also be able to claim for the cost of alternative accommodation from the other party.

Instructing searches

When you buy a property with a mortgage you will own that property, along with the lender. This means the lender will want your solicitor to conduct specific searches and complete certain checks before they will release your mortgage funds. If the lender in the future needs to repossess your house they will want to ensure they can do so without any issues attached to the property.

If you are buying using cash, you are not dictated to by a lender to request searches. However, for the sake of a few hundred pounds, purchasing the searches recommended by your solicitor could save you thousands if problems are found later.

The searches you need will depend on the location of your property, which is why it may be more advantageous, although not essential, to use a local solicitor.

The main searches which will be required as a minimum, no matter where your property is, are:

~ Local Authority Searches: there are two parts to a local authority search, LLC1 and CON29. The LLC1 (Local Land Charge Register search) covers any charges or attendant **restrictions relating to land or property.** It will review planning issues or if the property is a listed building, whether there are any building control issues, or pollution issues, such as if it is in a smoke control zone or conservation area.

~ The second part of the search is the CON29, which provides information relating to public **highways, proposals for new roads, rail schemes or planning decisions** that could affect the property, as well as outstanding statutory notices, breaches of planning or building regulations. It also checks if there is a compulsory purchase order in place. I had a client who had to sell her house due to the HS2 rail line. Unfortunately, she was unable to get the price she felt the house was worth so lost a lot of money, so you can see how important these searches are. Environmental factors, such as whether the house stands on contaminated land or in a radon gas affected area are also covered. I had a client who later found out the land his house was on wasn't treated properly from when it was a former waste disposal site, so his house was devalued drastically overnight.

~ Water and drainage searches: the local water company provides information on who owns and maintains the sewers, drains and piping. It confirms if the property is connected to a public water supply and the location of public sewers and drainage pipes. They will confirm if the water supply is rateable or metred and if in the future you plan to extend the property whether you need planning permission.

Other searches that may be recommended are as follows:

~ **Title searches, a title register and title plan:** This is purchased through the Land Registry and will be ordered by your solicitor. The title register will tell you who previously owned the property and what price they paid for it. It will state what charges or debts are registered against the property and give details about rights of way over the property.

~ **The title plan** is a map that will show the location of the property and provide boundaries relevant to the property.

~ **Environmental searches:** These searches can vary from one search provider to another but what must be considered by the Law Society is a report to establish if the property was built on contaminated land or near a landfill/waste management site.

~ **Flood risk report:** As its name suggests, this will provide a report highlighting the flood risk from the sea or a river. Also, with the increase of flooding from rainwater this is also highlighted in the report. This report is important as your property may not be insurable and be deemed high risk for the lenders to secure their money against. We have all seen the news reports in the last few years of people being flooded for the first time in increasingly frequent extreme weather events – don't assume your prospective property is safe from flooding! These reports are usually provided by the relevant local water company.

~ **Chancel repair liability search:** Chancel Repair Liability (CRL) is a financial obligation imposed on some property owners in England and Wales to pay for certain repairs to a church which may or may not be the local parish church. It may sound obscure and is most likely going to be irrelevant for most properties – however, it is still worth checking! It may not be mentioned in the title, but it is estimated half a million properties in England and Wales could be affected. If the property does have a chancel repair liability your solicitor can advise on a chancel indemnity insurance policy during the conveyancing process.

~ **Rivers Authority search (Canal and River search):** if you are purchasing a property that backs onto a river, canal or stream you will normally purchase the property with certain rights like fishing and mooring. You may also find yourself with financial responsibilities too, similar to the chancel repair liability.

~ **Commons registration search:** This search is normally used in rural areas to confirm if the property is being bought with land that is classed as 'common land' according to the Commons Registration Act 1965, which may mean other people have rights such as allowing their livestock to graze upon it or to collect wood.

~ **Coal mining report:** This provides information if there is a problem with the land in relation to historic mining. It will also report on any claims nearby due to properties being affected by mines. Most lenders will deem properties near mines unsuitable to secure lending on. However, some lenders such as building societies in mining towns may be able to offer security on the property, but the value of the property may be affected.

~ **Land Registry pre-completion searches:** These are made after exchange to make sure nothing has changed in regard to the property or your ability to purchase. They include a bankruptcy search, land charges search, and priority searches. Priority searches help you find whether anyone has made any charges or has any interest or rights on the property. It also clarifies the complete right of the seller to sell the property. Once the searches are returned clear you obtain a 'priority' title registration. This means no one can make any charges or rights on the property for 30 days from the time of the search.

Drawing up and execution of the mortgage documentation

This is required by the lender. The solicitor is responsible for drawing up the contract between the lender and the borrower. In England, this is called the Legal Charge. This is normally referred to as the mortgage deed.

The mortgage deed may take the form of a detailed document with all terms and conditions provided within it. Alternatively, it may be a single-page document stating that the parties agree to be bound by the terms and conditions of a mortgage applicable at the time. In this case the mortgage conditions booklet is issued as a separate document. These terms cannot be changed without the permission of both parties.

Other documents the solicitor may need to draw up are a deed of assignment whereby the lender establishes rights over a life assurance policy; and a guarantor contract if there is a guarantor. Some lenders want the guarantor to sign the title deed itself.

Finalising the finances

One of the last parts of the process is, of course, dealing with all financial aspects of the transactions, both the purchase and the mortgage. The solicitor needs to deal with the redemption of any existing mortgages owned by the purchaser – usually the sale of their current property will satisfy this.

The solicitor will request the money from the lender by issuing a certificate of title to the lender. They will then handle the funds, ensuring the balance meets the requirements. They will request your deposit and make sure that both funds add up to the purchase price of the property.

Your solicitor will also submit your payment of Stamp Duty Land Tax to Her Majesty's Revenue and Customs (HMRC).

Your solicitor will also deal with the payment of fees and charges for searches. They will usually bill you for this alongside their professional fees.

There are occasions where the solicitor will set down conditions for the advance, such as where the purchaser has declared they will pay off certain debts such as credit cards or unsecured loans using the mortgage funds. The solicitor will set aside the funds for paying the debts so that the transactions can complete ensuring the purchase was not reliant on the full advance which would leave no money to pay off the debts thus leaving the purchaser in higher debt than agreed in the contract.

SCAM ALERT! There have been many examples of incredibly sophisticated scams, where an email has appeared to be from a solicitor and is requesting the transfer of deposit funds, often tens of thousands of pounds, only for it to be a hacked email and the funds then disappear into the hands of scammers. Redress from the banks is not always guaranteed in these situations, so be extremely careful to receive the correct account and sort code information for the transfer of any funds!

Advice on outstanding issues

Although you are paying your solicitor to act on your behalf, they have a duty to advise both you and the lender when drawing up the mortgage.

The solicitor should advise the borrower on the consequences of signing the mortgage and be prepared to deal with any outstanding queries. The solicitor should also advise the lenders on any matters that may be relevant to the transaction. An example may be that a mine may be found near the property during the searches, and this will need to be presented to the lender to ensure they are still happy to use the property as security for the funds.

Lenders also expect the solicitor to be vigilant in respect of potential dangers and minimise the likelihood of fraud.

Exchanging contracts

During the exchange of contracts, normally both solicitors will read out the contracts over the phone in a recorded conversation to make sure the contracts are the same and then post them to each other. Once contracts have been exchanged, you are legally bound to buy the property. The solicitor will then tell the freeholder (if it's a leasehold property) you are the new owner, and check there has been a registered transfer of ownership with the Land Registry. If it is a share of a freehold purchase the solicitor will arrange for the new share certificate to be issued.

Completion date

Finally, we get to the ultimate aim of this book, which is to set a completion date whereby you finally get the keys to your new house. The estate agent will most likely hold the keys for you to pick up.

The day you complete, your solicitor will arrange for the money to be transferred to the seller's solicitor. If you are in a chain, ideally all the buyers and sellers in the chain will complete on the same day otherwise you may have to wait for the sellers to complete buying their new home before you can move in.

The time it takes from exchange to completion is decided by you and the seller but is usually a week. This can be affected by the chain of course so some negotiating within the chain may be required to set a completion date.

Practical things to do when moving house

Moving house, whether it be for the first time or the tenth, is rarely anyone's favourite task. In fact, it is said to be one of the most stressful life events you will undertake, even if it's the means to a better way of living. It is at this stage where most of your professional help ceases and you are left to it, but this stage of moving can be the most stressful if you haven't thought of everything. So here is a short guide for the practical side of things to think about when you are moving house. I have also put a checklist at the end for moving and a first night essential checklist.

Hand in your notice to your landlord

If you are currently renting, make sure you have contacted your landlord and confirmed your notice period. This could be just one or two months or if you have only just entered a six-month contract you may have to pay fees to exit the contract. Your tenancy agreement may have what is called a Break Clause, which is a provision that can be included in your lease agreement allowing you and your landlord to end the lease early if certain conditions are met. Make sure you know your preferred move date before handing in notice and think whether you want to keep the property for, say, another week, to give you time to move and possibly put right any repairs that could cost you your landlord's deposit.

Declutter and organise

It is very rare that you will have an occasion to handle every item you own in one event. Moving house is one such occasion. This is therefore the perfect time to get rid of anything you no longer need or haven't used for, say, twelve months. There are guides out there on how to declutter, but it can be an emotional thing to do. I love the twelve-month rule, that if I haven't used an item during that period or cannot remember using an item then I no longer need it. Also, think about what you want your new home to represent. If you are planning to start a family it may be that all that stuff in your man cave could go to better use, or if you are downsizing now the kids have moved out, can you recycle or give away furniture from the kids' rooms? If you are using a removal company, they ask for an estimate on how many items you plan to move, so a good sort out will help you with this and set you up to a good start in the new house.

Children and pets

Depending on your circumstances, this could be the biggest consideration of all. Are your children going to need to change schools? This is of course not a simple process, especially if there are no places in your preferred choice of school. If they are staying in their current school, then you just need to update the school with your new address and possibly new doctor's details. Another logistical consideration for children and pets: do you need to organise a carer for the day so you can focus on the move rather than the safety and whereabouts of children and pets. If you don't have any childcare options, do you need to move on a school day? If your pets are going into a kennel, is there availability or any specific conditions you need to be aware of.

Update your details with third parties

The list of third parties you may need to update with your new address and contact details can be extensive, depending on your circumstances. However, this can be broken down into two categories, Important/ Compliant and Social. Prioritise your important/compliant list as this will be all the third parties who you must update. Once these have been contacted, then update those on your social list.

Important/compliant list

~ The local authority for Council Tax purposes

~ Your employer

~ Your utility companies (gas, electric, water)

~ Yor GP and dentist

~ Schools

~ Phone and internet providers

~ Your bank

~ The DVLA

~ TV Licencing

~ Inland Revenue

~ Electoral Role

~ Insurance providers.

Important! Confirm you have paid all final bills

I have met with many clients who have had their final bill for electric, water, phone etc sent to their previous address and have missed it as they no longer lived there. This has then led to a default on the account which immediately puts a black mark on that credit rating! In some cases, this has meant they have struggled to get finance following their move. They knew nothing about it. This is important! As a safety net, ensure you have subscribed to a mail forwarding service with Royal Mail, for at least three months.

Social list

~ Memberships: this could be anything from sports clubs, children's clubs or associations. Remember, you may have completed important next of kin details which in an emergency will need to be correct if you are to be contacted quickly.

~ Store cards, online shops, magazine subscription etc need to be updated.

~ Friends and family. I am sure your close friends and family will know that you are moving but you may have an aunt or uncle somewhere who sends a cheque at Christmas once a year. Don't let their details get into the wrong hands just because you didn't update them with your contact details.

Route planner and van hire

You may need to hire a van as part of the removal process. If you don't drive a van every day, you may feel a little wary driving down tight roads or even on motorways, so plan your route. Which side does the van open so you know which way to pull up to the house? How much does it cost and does your licence allow you to drive the size of vehicle you plan to drive? How long are you hiring it for and what help will you have with you? You may have four people helping but only two seats in the car or van so how will your help be transported?

Pack up and mark up

Ideally, you need to start packing up two weeks before the move date. This may seem too early but by giving yourself two weeks to pack most non-essentials this will give you time to organise and label everything properly. This will make life much easier and less stressful when you unpack at the new home. You want to make the labels big and easy to read so if someone helps you later in the day who wasn't there in the morning, they will easily understand what is in a box and where it belongs in the new house. This will also help reduce double handling boxes as they can be delivered directly to the room in which they belong.

You also want to start thinking about reducing the food in your cupboards and freezer. If you are defrosting the freezer as you are taking it with you, think about how long it takes to do so.

Confirm completion date with solicitor

Again, two weeks before the move, confirm the completion date with your solicitor as this will be the green light to start packing.

Keep your valuables safe

This might seem obvious but it's surprising how easily your valuables can be misplaced. Also, you will be leaving front doors open when loading and unloading, and car and van doors will be left unattended during the move. Things like your passports, driving licences and paperwork can be kept in a folder and locked in the glove box or left at a relative's house. You may be happy putting them in a box labelled for the office. Jewellery and larger items will want to be packed safely but possibly not labelled up to give opportunist thieves the chance to steal them. Again, you could leave these at a relative's house or place them in the bedroom box. Just know where they are to save confusion and anxiety looking for them once the move is complete.

The day before the move

You may feel a little stressed or overwhelmed the day before the move. You are going to need to pack some essential items that need to be marked clearly for your first night in the new house. Most importantly, make sure you put your mobile phone on charge.

Move all your boxes, or as many as you can, downstairs to start clearing out rooms ready for a final walk around to make sure nothing has been missed. Don't forget your loft!

Things to pack for your first night in your new home, the night before if you can:

For you
- ~ Bedding
- ~ Toilet paper
- ~ Toiletries for the whole family: toothpaste, toothbrush, shampoo, conditioner
- ~ Hand soap
- ~ Towel for each family member
- ~ Pyjamas for whole family
- ~ Work clothes
- ~ First aid kit

For the kids
- ~ Bedding/travel cot
- ~ Favourite toy if necessary
- ~ Change of clothes
- ~ Entertainment: iPad/laptop/charger, headphones, crayons/ colouring book, few toys
- ~ Night light

For the pets

- ~ Pet food
- ~ Lead/collar (update the address)
- ~ Toys
- ~ Food and water bowls
- ~ Litter box/waste bags
- ~ Bed/cage
- ~ Any medication

To eat

- ~ Paper plates/cups
- ~ Basic cutlery
- ~ Dinner (or takeaway menu!)
- ~ Breakfast items
- ~ Snacks
- ~ Water
- ~ Kettle, tea/coffee, filters, mugs, milk, squash
- ~ Corkscrew/bottle opener/something bubbly
- ~ Tin opener

For cleaning and DIY

- ~ Basic cleaning supplies/rubber gloves
- ~ Bin liners
- ~ Screwdriver/hammer/pliers/scissors
- ~ Torch/lightbulbs
- ~ Phone charger
- ~ Extension cable
- ~ Pen and paper
- ~ Paper towels/wet wipes

On the day of the move

Check your meter readings, gas, electric and water and write them down. You will need these details when you cancel your utilities. It is always good practice to take a photo with your phone.

Empty each room and then have a good look around – have you taken all the pictures down, have you checked the bathroom cupboards for toiletries or medication you may need? Is the garage empty and have you any outbuildings that need to be emptied?

Once the house is empty you will need to hand your keys over, whether to the landlord or the estate agents you sold through. Before you do, say goodbye to any neighbours who you may not see again. Finally, take a photo outside your house as this will be the last time you will be there as owners or occupiers. Do the same when you get to your new house. Social media pops up with memories each year and this will be a wonderful memory to look back on, even if it's stressful. When you look back you will remember all the happy thoughts and laugh about all the mishaps.

Your new home!

You've now completed the long and complicated journey to your new home. You've chosen the property you wanted to buy, you were successful in securing your position as the buyer, you've navigated your way through the negotiations with the vendor, and, crucially, you have obtained the optimum way to purchase it with the mortgage that best suits you, your circumstances and this property purchase. You've drawn up and used all the checklists and you've moved in without forgetting the dog!

Phew, you and your family are now in the home you have spent months working towards securing. Hopefully, with help in some small way from this book, it has all gone without a hitch, or if there have been bumps in the road along the way, you have now had the knowledge to know how to overcome them.

I consider myself really lucky in that I help people buy their homes. Homes where families are started, homes where relationships are grown. I really hope this book has guided you and taken some of the stress and uncertainty away that comes with buying a house.

Good luck with this next part of your life in your new home!

Moving Checklist

Two months before completion date

☐ Organise van hire/removal company

☐ Buy cardboard boxes and packaging such as bubble wrap and paper

☐ Start decluttering/donating unwanted items/take a trip to the tip

☐ Start packing unessential items

☐ Organise pet care such as kennels.

One month before completion date

☐ If you are moving far away get your car serviced or check your oil and water levels and tyre pressures at least

☐ Register with your new doctors and dentist if required

☐ Inform your local council of your change of address and cancel payments

☐ Inform your phone and internet providers of your change of address

☐ Inform the DVLA and request new driving licence with new address

☐ Notify your bank with your change of address

☐ Update your insurance providers and ensure you have buildings insurance organised for exchange date

☐ Start packing items you don't use every day, ensuring you label the boxes as you fill them

☐ Arrange childcare if necessary

Two weeks before completion

☐ Organise your mail and redirect for at least 3 months. This will ensure any final bills are sent to you and are not missed

☐ Clean your house as you go, it will help you not miss anything

☐ Tell your friends and family your new address details, inform mail order companies, newspapers and magazine deliveries.

One week before completion

☐ If exchanged, make sure your buildings and contents insurance has been set up, as you are now liable for the property and to complete the transaction.

☐ Confirm with the solicitor the completion date is still the same as planned

☐ Notify TV Licensing of new address

☐ Your packing should be close to completion

☐ Speak with your neighbours to ensure there is room outside your house to move ie park a lorry or van and manoeuvre large furniture without causing damage

☐ Empty and defrost the fridge and freezer

☐ Empty your kitchen cupboards

☐ Pack valuable and important documents in a safe place and remember where you plan to keep them

☐ Remind friends and family helping with the move of times and dates and that they will still be there

Things to do on moving day

☐ Record all utility bills and take a photo of the meter readings. Let your providers know you are moving today

☐ Strip the beds and pack with your first night essentials

☐ Check the bathrooms for toiletries and medication

Add additional items for the list

☐

☐

☐

☐

☐

About the Author

Tom Archer is a licensed mortgage adviser who thrives on helping first-time buyers take their first step into property ownership.

Tom served in the Grenadier Guards and the Parachute Regiment, and it was during this time that he decided he wanted to know more about buying property but just didn't know where to start.

Tom bought his first house when he was 19 and he has since gone on to buy others, some with and some without professional help... and made loads of mistakes along the way. By becoming a qualified mortgage adviser, Tom was finally able to understand the whole process. And he discovered a passion for helping other people to avoid the potential pitfalls in the house-buying process. All that knowledge and experience is distilled into this, Tom's first book.

Tom loves spending time with his wife, son and daughter. He is a keen runner and cyclist and has recently started his journey into the world of triathlons.

Milton Keynes UK
Ingram Content Group UK Ltd.
UKHW022058031023
429886UK00010B/756